sexual dilemmas provide us a treasure trove of the erotic, playful, sensual ways to grow, adapt, and accommodate sex in relationships throughout a couple's life.

McCarthy reminds us that sexual desire can be responsive, that cultural changes influence couples' expectations and wants in their sexual lives and he invites us to figure it out, talk about sex, and share in the journey to finding what is pleasurable for each partner.

Thank goodness for his remarkable history as a couples sex therapist and writer about sex. We can trust his advice and we can gain confidence and hope in his steady reassurance that sexual sharing can be created and enjoyed by most couples.

He reminds us that going the distance as a couple involves 'all the senses'—including hearing each other, touching with openness and trust, collaborating to build sexual sharing. Hearing, touching, collaborating inevitably leads to couples finding their own sexual voice."

**Sallie Foley**, sex therapist and author

"Barry and Emily McCarthy give practical, reassuring, knowledgeable, and wise suggestions for living a partnered life with satisfaction, security and sexuality. They write for everyone whether monogamous, monogamish, polyamorous, pansexual, straight, gay, bi, or more. Their point is that sex is good for us, our lives, our relationships, adding 15 to 20% to our satisfaction. Their plain, clear writing helps people decide what is right for them and their relationships so that their relationship agreements can promote desire/pleasure/eroticism/satisfaction. Whether you are a therapist, client, or student wanting clarity on what works and doesn't work in significant relationships involving sexual expression, *Enhancing Couple Sexuality* will be an important contribution to your thinking."

**Susan E. Stiritz, MBA, PhD, MSW**, AASECT president, associate professor of practice, chair of the specialization in Sexual Health and Education, The Brown School, Washington University, St. Louis

"Barry and Emily, co-authors of 14 books, are themselves skillful, cherishing and have a positive sexual relationship of 52 years. In their book they encourage each person, of any sexual orientation, to be their 'authentic sexual self', affirming healthy sexuality, at any age, whether you are married, partnered, divorced, single, or widowed. Rich with information and case examples, as well as providing many thoughtful exercises, this book is a must read for all those who want to feel connected and have a joyous sexual relationship."

**Clare E. Mézes, MSc, RP, RMFT**, Individual, Couple, Sex and Family Therapy

"This is an incredible book – easy to read, couple friendly, and evidence based. So many individuals would benefit from reading this thoughtful manuscript before and after establishing relationships."

**R. Taylor Segraves, MD**, editor, *Journal of Sex and Marital Therapy*

"Team McCarthy does it again! Their outstanding book promoting healthy sexuality with scientifically and clinically validated psychological, biological/medical, and social/relational information will be valued highly by the public and professionals alike."

**Michael A. Perelman, PhD**, co-director, Human Sexuality Continuing Education Program, clinical professor emeritus of Psychology in Psychiatry, founder & chairman MAP Education & Research Foundation

"Barry and Emily McCarthy make an important contribution to the field of sex and couples research and therapy by discussing sexual relationships in the context of couple relationships. Therapists, heterosexual couples, whether traditional or not-so-traditional, and gay or lesbian couples in monogamous or consensually non-monogamous relationships, will find a lot of value in this new book. Sexual myths are debunked, psycho-sexual exercises offered, couple cases discussed and a range of sensitive issues are considered."

**Jennifer Fitzgerald, PhD**, University of Queensland, Brisbane, Australia

"In plain language the McCarthys give us the recipe for the secret sauce that makes sex pleasurable in long-term relationships. Readers will learn that with equal measures of wisdom and sensitivity, a dash of spice, and some gentle stirring even relationships that have cooled can simmer again."

**Kathryn Hall, PhD**, president, Society for Sex Therapy and Research; co-editor of *Principles and Practice of Sex Therapy*

"*Finding Your Sexual Voice* is my top pick for a great book about sex for couples. McCarthy engages couples with thoughtfulness, warmth, and reassuring guidance. He is a leader in the field of sexual health and creating better sex for couples is his lifelong passion—one couple, one book at a time. In *Finding Your Sexual Voice*, he provides up-to-date research on sexual functioning, neuroplasticity and sexual response, as well as attachment and attunement as part of sexuality. His practical approaches solving

# ENHANCING COUPLE SEXUALITY

Sexuality is multi-causal and multi-dimensional, with large individual, couple, cultural, and value differences. Each person and couple deserve to experience sexuality as a positive factor in their lives and relationships. *Enhancing Couple Sexuality* is an accessible guide that will help you to explore couple sexuality, with a focus on promoting healthy sexuality and overcoming sexual dysfunction, conflict, and avoidance.

The couple challenge, regardless of relationship status or sexual orientation, is to integrate intimacy and eroticism into your relationship, while reinforcing the new sexual mantra of desire/pleasure/eroticism/satisfaction. Healthy sexuality is a combination of responsibility for your authentic sexual self and being an intimate sexual team. Each chapter in this book presents scientifically-validated guidelines, a compelling case study, and a psychosexual skill exercise to make every concept personal and concrete.

*Enhancing Couple Sexuality* will motivate and empower couples to create and maintain a satisfying, secure, and sexual relationship. Whether you are married or dating, 25 or 65, this valuable resource will provide strategies to enhance your sexual relationship now and in the future.

**Barry McCarthy** is a professor of psychology at American University, a diplomate in clinical psychology, a diplomate in sex therapy, and a certified couple therapist. He has published over 115 professional articles, 32 book chapters, and 20 books. He has presented over 450 professional workshops nationally and internationally. In 2016, he received the SSTAR Masters and Johnson award for lifetime contributions to the sex therapy field.

**Emily McCarthy** received a BS degree in speech communication, and her writing and wisdom provides a balanced, humanistic perspective. This is Emily and Barry's 14th co-authored book.

# ENHANCING COUPLE SEXUALITY
Creating an Intimate and Erotic Bond

*Barry McCarthy and
Emily McCarthy*

NEW YORK AND LONDON

First published 2019
by Routledge
52 Vanderbilt Avenue, New York, NY 10017

and by Routledge
2 Park Square, Milton Park, Abingdon, Oxon, OX14 4RN

*Routledge is an imprint of the Taylor & Francis Group, an informa business*

© 2019 Taylor & Francis

The rights of Barry McCarthy and Emily McCarthy to be identified as authors of this work has been asserted by them in accordance with sections 77 and 78 of the Copyright, Designs and Patents Act 1988.

All rights reserved. No part of this book may be reprinted or reproduced or utilized in any form or by any electronic, mechanical, or other means, now known or hereafter invented, including photocopying and recording, or in any information storage or retrieval system, without permission in writing from the publishers.

*Trademark notice*: Product or corporate names may be trademarks or registered trademarks, and are used only for identification and explanation without intent to infringe.

*Library of Congress Cataloging-in-Publication Data*
Names: McCarthy, Barry W., 1943– author. | McCarthy, Emily J., author.
Title: Enhancing couple sexuality : creating an intimate and erotic bond /
Barry McCarthy and Emily McCarthy.
Description: New York, NY : Routledge, 2019. | Includes bibliographical references.
Identifiers: LCCN 2018061594 (print) | LCCN 2019001306 (ebook) |
ISBN 9780429446092 (E-book) | ISBN 9781138333215 (hardback) |
ISBN 9781138333222 (pbk.) | ISBN 9780429446092 (ebk)
Subjects: LCSH: Couples—Sexual behavior. | Sexual excitement. |
Sex in marriage. | Sex therapy.
Classification: LCC HQ31 (ebook) | LCC HQ31 .M138 2019 (print) |
DDC 306.7—dc23
LC record available at https://lccn.loc.gov/2018061594

ISBN: 978-1-138-33321-5 (hbk)
ISBN: 978-1-138-33322-2 (pbk)
ISBN: 978-0-429-44609-2 (ebk)

Typeset in Perpetua
by Apex CoVantage, LLC

# CONTENTS

| | | |
|---|---|---|
| 1 | Sex Myths: Old and New | 1 |
| 2 | The New Sexual Mantra | 19 |
| 3 | Psychobiosocial Model for Understanding and Change | 33 |
| 4 | Female—Male Sexual Equity | 45 |
| 5 | Dimensions of Touch, Pleasure, and Sexuality | 59 |
| 6 | Good Enough Sex (GES) | 73 |
| 7 | Integrating Intimacy and Eroticism | 85 |
| 8 | Your Couple Sexual Style | 99 |
| 9 | Personal Responsibility/Intimate Sexual Team | 113 |
| 10 | The Paradox of Sexuality | 127 |
| 11 | Vulnerabilities and Challenges | 141 |
| 12 | Sexuality and Aging | 157 |
| 13 | Sexually, One Size Never Fits All | 171 |

14  Monogamy vs. Consensual Non-Monogamy                        185

*Appendix A: Choosing a Sex, Couple, or Individual Therapist*    201
*Appendix B: Suggested Readings*                                 203
*References*                                                     205

# 1

# SEX MYTHS: OLD AND NEW

The world of sexuality is shrouded by myths. Sex myths are powerful, destructive, and die hard. The old myths are based on repressive attitudes and sexual ignorance. The new myths are based on unrealistic performance demands and erotic perfectionism.

Myths interfere with developing and maintaining a satisfying, secure, and sexual relationship. We want to motivate and empower you to create a healthy sexual relationship. Knowledge is power. Since the publication of the Masters and Johnson classic text *Human Sexual Inadequacy* in 1970 the field of sex therapy and couple sexuality has discovered scientifically validated information to help individuals and couples embrace sexuality (Binik & Hall, 2014). Unfortunately, these understandings have not been accepted in the culture and some have resulted in new sex myths.

This book is focused on helping married and partnered couples to understand themselves, each other, and their relationship so that sexuality has a positive role in your life.

To begin, let's see how much you know about sexuality. Take ten minutes to individually complete this quiz. Don't worry about performance anxiety, it won't be graded. Don't give the socially desirable answer, but what you really believe.

### True—False Sex Assessment

1. The major predictor of marital success is love and communication.
2. Sexually, the happiest time is the first six months of marriage.

3. The honeymoon is a wonderful way to start a marriage, especially sexually.
4. Having a baby during the first year of marriage enhances marital satisfaction and stability.
5. Couples who establish a good premarital sexual relationship find marital sex requires little additional effort.
6. Traditional sex roles are the most satisfying for both the man and woman.
7. Affection is primarily the woman's domain and intercourse the man's domain.
8. There is strong empirical support for the concept that "Men are from Mars and Women are from Venus".
9. Planning a child reduces sexual fun and spontaneity.
10. Same-sex friends give the most honest, helpful advice about marriage and marital sex.
11. Having a child strengthens a fragile marriage.
12. The male should be the sexual initiator.
13. Seeking couple therapy, sex therapy, or a marital enhancement workshop is an indication of major marital problems.
14. The birth of a planned, wanted child heralds a period of increased couple intimacy.
15. Most affairs occur after ten years of marriage.
16. Most divorces occur after ten years of marriage.
17. Intercourse lasts between 10–30 minutes; less than five minutes indicates premature ejaculation.
18. Over 90% of women have orgasm during intercourse, i.e. vaginal orgasm.
19. "G" spot orgasm and multiple orgasms are the most satisfying.
20. Pain during intercourse is rare and is usually a symptom of relational alienation.
21. A couple with a good marriage and good sex are immune from extramarital affairs.
22. Intimacy-based couple therapy almost always enhances sexual desire, especially erotic feelings.

23. Successfully treated couples have no need for a relapse prevention plan.
24. When there is a history of sexual trauma, trauma issues must be addressed before couple sexuality issues.
25. Couples who cohabitate before marriage, especially longer than two years, experience better sex and less divorce.

Add the number of trues you checked. The average number for the public is 8.5 and for health professionals is 4.5. In fact, this is a sex myth test—they are all false. Remember, knowledge is power. Let's examine scientifically and personally relevant information which is empowering and motivating.

1. Love and communication are important, but the best predictor of marital (relational) success is your ability to deal with differences and conflicts. The paradox is that sex cannot save a marriage, but sexual conflicts and problems can destroy a relationship. Neither love nor communication are enough to resolve sexual problems. You need to directly address sexual problems and conflicts.
2. Most couples experience a limerance phase (romantic love/passionate sex/idealization). Limerance is a wonderful experience, but it's fragile and time-limited (usually six months to a year—seldom two years). Limerance is usually gone by the time of marriage. For most couples, the first year of marriage is challenging and stressful with reduced marital and sexual satisfaction (McCarthy & McCarthy, 2004).
3. Most couples need three to six months to develop a couple sexual style to replace the limerance phase. The honeymoon is not the time or place to do this. Honeymoon sex is burdened by unrealistic expectations and performance pressure. Many couples wish they had delayed their honeymoon for a year after the marriage so they could enjoy this special time, including sexually.
4. The science is clear. The wise decision is to wait two years before having a planned, wanted child (McCarthy & McCarthy, 2004). Use that time to create a respectful, trusting, emotionally committed

marriage and a couple sexual style featuring strong, resilient sexual desire. Most couples decide to have children, but an unplanned pregnancy or having children before you are ready can subvert your relationship.
5. The vast majority of couples are sexual before marriage. The limerance phase is a fantastic way to start as a sexual couple. The challenge is to create a couple sexual style; you cannot return to the limerance phase. A sad statistic is that 40% of couples say their best sex was the first six months of the relationship. They did not meet the challenge to develop a couple sexual style (McCarthy & McCarthy, 2009).
6. Although some couples thrive with traditional sex roles, most prefer a flexible, equitable relationship and resent the rigidity of traditional male—female roles. An equitable relationship allows you to be a fully functioning person and choose the sexual roles and values that are the right fit for you and your relationship. An equitable relationship makes it easier to be intimate and erotic allies.
7. The traditional split of women valuing affection and men valuing intercourse subverts couple sexuality. Affection is valuable for the man, woman, and couple. Intercourse is valuable for the woman, man, and couple. Healthy couple sexuality is not split by gender. Sexuality is more satisfying when both partners value affection and intercourse. Both partners have the right to initiate and both have the right to say no to sex.
8. "Pop sex" beliefs are a major cause of confusion and conflict. Simple rules sound good, but are destructive for real life couple sexuality. A key for sexual desire and satisfaction is to view your partner as your intimate sexual friend. In adult relationships, there are many more psychological, relational, and sexual similarities than differences between women and men (Hyde, 2005).
9. Planned, wanted children are the ideal. Sex with the goal of pregnancy is an aphrodisiac. You've spent years using contraception to prevent pregnancy so sex with the goal of pregnancy is special. Fun and spontaneity is great, but enjoy planned sex with the desire to create a child. Sex to create a family is special.

10. Myths and conflicts are often supported by same gender friends. Jokes and gender stereotypes are reinforced by friends who try to be helpful, but in fact, reinforce myths and self-defeating approaches to gender. They offer simplistic and destructive advice based on attacking and blaming the opposite gender partner. Self-help and same gender advice is based on "pop sex", not scientifically validated information. This encourages people to make "emotional choices" rather than "wise decisions". A wise sexual decision means it makes sense emotionally and practically and works in the short and long term.
11. All marriages go through good and bad times. A healthy marriage is satisfying, secure, and sexual. Ideally, you establish a satisfying and secure relationship before having a child. Fear and negative motivation drives emotional choices. People get pregnant with the hope that a child will save a fragile marriage. In fact, the most common time both married and partnered couples break up is 6 months before or after the birth of a child. We are pro-child, but a child does not save a fragile relationship. Positive motivation promotes wise relational and sexual decisions.
12. In most cultures, including the United States, males are the sexual initiators. This is based on adolescent and young adult socialization related to spontaneous erections. It is not a healthy model for adults, especially those who are married or partnered. The problem with men being the sex initiator is it traps the woman in the sexual gatekeeper role and the couple in the traditional power struggle over intercourse frequency. This devalues pleasure-oriented touching and breaks down into "intercourse=sex" and "intercourse or nothing" struggles. In the equity model either partner can initiate and either partner can say no. Each partner can initiate a sensual, playful, or erotic experience rather than sex being narrowly defined as intercourse. Sensual, playful, and erotic scenarios are sexual (Kleinplatz, 2010). Believing the man should initiate based on a spontaneous erection ultimately subverts sexual desire and satisfaction. With aging the man has fewer spontaneous erections so the couple have less sex.

13. One of the best decisions you make as a couple is to use all your resources to empower sexuality. The decision to enter couple therapy, sex therapy, or attend a marital enhancement workshop (especially if sexuality is a topic) is a sign of strength, not weakness. It says that you and your partner are motivated to maintain a satisfying, secure, and sexual relationship. Rather than dealing with a problem in the acute phase, couples delay seeking help until the sexual problem is chronic and severe. Instead of remaining stuck in the cycle of alienation and blame—counter-blame, focus on creating desire/pleasure/eroticism/satisfaction. This is a team project. Be intimate and erotic friends in addressing problems and creating a couple sexual style.
14. A baby is a major challenge for each parent, their relationship, and couple sexuality. For most couples, pregnancy and parenting negatively impacts sexuality. You have less time, energy, and are sleep deprived. Babies have a great need for affection and caring touch. For 70% of couples, sexual frequency and satisfaction goes down and stays down after the birth of children (Ahlborg, 2008). If you want to be in the 30% of couples who maintain sexual desire and satisfaction while parenting, approach this as an intimate team challenge. Rather than trying to convince or coerce your partner, work together as a parenting team and as a sexual team. Affirm the value of touching with awareness that sexuality can have a range of roles, meanings, and outcomes.
15. The issue of affairs (EMAs) is one of the most value-laden and contentious in the relationship and sexuality fields. The last chapter of this book presents a detailed exploration of monogamy vs. consensual non-monogamy. The most common time for an EMA is the first five years of marriage. An EMA is a major cause of break-up in marital and partnered relationships (Gordon, Baucom & Snyder, 2004). Couples typically do not have a specific dialogue about EMAs, especially their personal, relational, and situational vulnerabilities to an EMA. In terms of sexual health, prevention is always the best strategy. This is particularly true of couples who have non-traditional values about EMAs (those who adopt consensual non-monogamy).

Whether traditional or non-traditional, almost no one supports secret EMAs, which is by far the most common pattern.

16. Of marriages which eventually end in divorce, almost 40% end in the first five years. The major cause of break-up early in a marriage is a sexual problem—sexual dysfunction, sexual conflicts (especially about EMAs), and sexual avoidance (Fine & Harvey, 2006). The early years of marriage are not a problem-free "honeymoon". Rather they are a time of dialogue and work to establish a satisfying and secure bond and a couple sexual style to replace the limerance phase. There are fatally flawed marriages that never should have happened, but usually a divorce is caused by not dealing with the challenge of creating a satisfying, secure, and sexual marriage. Instead they relied on the cultural myth that divorce occurs after ten years or longer.

17. The average sexual encounter is between 15–45 minutes of which three to seven minutes involves intercourse (Althof, 2014). Few couples have intercourse which extends to 12 minutes. Premature ejaculation involves intercourse of less than two minutes and the man does not feel in control of when he ejaculates. The myth of intercourse length is another example of unrealistic sex performance demands. Intercourse is the natural continuation of the pleasuring/eroticism process rather than an individual pass—fail performance test.

18. The myth of vaginal vs. clitoral orgasm has existed since Freud. Physiologically an orgasm is an orgasm, whether from manual, oral, intercourse, rubbing, masturbation, or vibrator stimulation. Only one in seven women orgasm the same way as men—a single orgasm during intercourse not needing additional stimulation. One in three women is never or almost never orgasmic during intercourse. This is not a sex dysfunction—it is a normal variation of female sexual response. Two in three women can be orgasmic during intercourse, usually involving multiple stimulation before and during intercourse (Graham, 2014).

19. The major cause of female secondary non-orgasmic response is unrealistic performance demands. Some women enjoy "G-spot" stimulation to orgasm and some have a multi-orgasmic response pattern. However, there is no scientific evidence that multi-orgasmic response

or "G-spot" orgasm is more satisfying. The key for satisfaction is to accept your orgasmic pattern ("orgasmic voice").

20. Painful sex (dyspareunia) is a very common female problem. Sexual pain is an example of the importance for the psychobiosocial model of sexual assessment and treatment. It is more likely that relationship alienation is a side effect of sexual pain rather than a cause of sexual pain. Sexual pain is best understood and treated as a couple issue. The man is her intimate and erotic friend, rather than someone to perform for. The focus is increased sexual comfort and pleasure rather than totally pain-free intercourse.

21. We are strong advocates for healthy marriages and satisfying sexuality, but that does not make you immune from an extra-marital affair (EMA). EMAs are an example of sexual behavior being multi-causal, multi-dimensional with large individual, couple, cultural, and value differences. The most common cause of EMAs is high opportunity. A prevention strategy is to have a specific dialogue about psychological, situational, and mood vulnerabilities for an EMA. You make an agreement that if the partner is in a high-risk situation, he will discuss the impact of a potential EMA before it occurs (this is equally true for the woman).

22. Intimacy-based couple therapy is of great value in creating a secure attachment bond and dealing with differences and conflicts. However, couple sexuality is more than intimacy and security. The challenge, whether married or partnered, straight or gay, is to integrate intimacy and eroticism into your relationship (Perel, 2006). Eroticism is a very different dimension than intimacy, but is not incompatible or adversarial. Eroticism is a crucial dimension in the mantra of desire/pleasure/eroticism/satisfaction.

23. The most demoralized couples are those who changed and then relapse. Should you blame yourself, your partner, or your relationship? When we learn the therapist didn't help the couple create an individualized relapse prevention plan we say blame the therapist. Sexuality cannot rest on its laurels, you need an individualized relapse prevention plan to ensure you maintain sexual gains and grow as a sexual couple.

24. Negative sexual experiences in childhood, adolescence, or young adulthood are almost universal. Sadly, sexual trauma (child sexual abuse, incest, and rape) is very frequent for both females and males. In most cases, addressing trauma issues in the context of couple sexuality is the best strategy. The core of sexual trauma is the adult or older adolescent's (almost always male) sexual wants override the emotional needs of the child. In working with couples dealing with a trauma history, the survivor has the power of veto with confidence that your partner will honor the veto (the opposite of what occurred in sexual abuse). Part of recovery is developing a sexual voice which values desire/pleasure/eroticism/satisfaction. You have not just survived trauma, but can thrive personally, relationally, and sexually (Maltz, 2012).
25. Most Americans cohabitate before marriage, especially those who marry in their late 20s or 30s. Contrary to "common sense" beliefs, cohabitating couples have higher rates of sexual problems and divorce. What makes a good cohabitation relationship is not what makes a good marriage. Sexual problems are a major cause of divorce among couples who cohabitated. They have higher rates of EMAs and lower sexual frequency after two years of the relationship. Instead of sexuality having a positive role of energizing your bond and reinforcing feelings of desire and desirability, sexual conflicts and avoidance drain your relationship. Cohabitating couples need to devote time and energy to create a satisfying and secure marriage and a couple sexual style which integrates intimacy and eroticism.

## Megan and Connor

Megan and Connor had been married less than two years and were threatening divorce. They had been a romantic love/passionate sex/idealized couple who were embarrassed and blaming about the non-sexual state of their marriage. Luckily, they had a supportive family, especially Connor's older sister, who assured them that relational and sexual problems are common in the early years of marriage. She strongly urged them to consult a licensed marriage therapist with a specialty in sexual problems. A very wise decision.

The therapist conducted a four-session assessment. They met as a couple for the initial session. This provided a strong message that relational and sexual problems are best addressed and treated as a couple issue. Connor found this particularly helpful because he felt Megan and her friends treated him as the "bad guy". Although both spouses were well-educated (Megan has a BA and Connor an MA), they were influenced by "pop psych" and "pop sex" simplistic slogans. The therapist suggested they read a chapter from *Rekindling Desire* to give them a scientifically validated understanding of relational and sexual issues (McCarthy & McCarthy, 2014). At first Connor was hesitant, but in reading and discussing with Megan he admitted that many of their problems were myth-based. What was particularly striking was Connor's low expectations of marital sex. On the other extreme, Megan had unrealistic expectations that love and intimacy would resolve everything. No wonder their marriage was in so much trouble—they were not speaking the same relational and sexual language.

The therapist was empathic and respectful, but clear that the marriage was in major trouble. In conducting the individual psychological/relational/sexual histories (sessions two and three), she emphasized the importance of being truthful about personal and sexual vulnerabilities. If the histories were conducted with the spouse in the room, the therapist would receive a socially desirable "sanitized" version rather than a genuine narrative.

The fourth session was a 90-minute couple meeting which bridged the assessment and treatment phases. There were three focuses:

1. Create a genuine narrative about Megan and Connor's psychological/relational/sexual strengths and vulnerabilities.
2. Agree to a six-month "good faith" effort to create a satisfying and secure marriage while developing a new couple sexual style.
3. Begin the change process by engaging in the first psychosexual skill exercise focused on sexual comfort (done in the privacy of their home).

The therapeutic strategy was to confront sexual myths and replace these with a motivating, empowering understanding of couple sexuality. Megan and Connor had been unaware of how sexual myths had undermined their marriage. Megan's magical beliefs in love and communication as the answer to any differences and conflicts had set her and the relationship up for feeling demoralized when the magic didn't work. Connor's assumptions that he didn't have to build the marriage and that sex should remain in the limerance phase contributed to their problems. When the therapist said they needed to discuss and decide on the right relational style, and then the right couple sexual style, it was as if she was speaking a different language. That was the analogy the therapist used—instead of the traditional gender war language Megan and Connor needed to speak the same relational and sexual language. Megan needed to be realistic in acceptance of herself, Connor, and the strengths and vulnerabilities of their relationship. The challenge for Connor was to raise expectations of marriage, put time and energy into dealing with Megan, and develop a couple sexual style which integrated intimacy and eroticism.

In the "both—and" approach, Megan and Connor focused on intimacy, pleasuring, and eroticism in an integrated manner. Especially important was Connor emphasizing sexual involvement and pleasure, not just intercourse frequency. The therapist urged them to develop a couple sexual style with "sex worth having". Rather than hoping to return to the limerance phase, Megan and Connor committed to a new couple sexual style. A major learning for Connor was that Megan's satisfaction was not controlled by orgasm. At her request, he stopped asking "did you come?" Instead, he turned toward her and was actively involved in giving and receiving pleasure-oriented touching before and during intercourse as well as in afterplay. He did this for himself, not to please Megan. A core factor for Megan was that Connor remain present throughout lovemaking rather than being so goal-oriented.

They developed a Complementary couple sexual style which reinforced strong, resilient sexual desire. Rather than the traditional power struggles which split sex, with Megan emphasizing intimacy and pleasure and Connor emphasizing eroticism and intercourse, both valued desire/pleasure/eroticism/satisfaction. Megan and Connor adopted the Best

Friend relational style and the Complementary couple sexual style. This was a challenge for Megan who felt they should have the same sexual and relational styles (a common mistaken assumption).

Connor embraced positive expectations about the marriage and marital sexuality. Megan had a strong belief in a flawless marital relationship leading to dramatic, perfect sex. As a young adult, she was overly influenced by "pop sex", especially Cosmopolitan magazine. The therapist did not put Megan down, but did challenge her to adopt positive, realistic, personally relevant marital and sexual expectations. By far the hardest issue was to confront the belief that if Connor really loved her, he would instinctively know what she wanted sexually (the sexual mind reader myth).

The therapist assigned a psychosexual skill exercise to clearly state what each found most attractive about the spouse and make two or three requests which would increase the spouse's attractiveness. The best time to talk about sex (in addition to a therapist's office) is the day before being sexual. Connor and Megan would talk on the porch over one or two glasses of wine (not a bottle) and make clear, personal requests of scenarios and techniques they wanted to try the next day. These were requests, not demands. The most important guideline for Megan was making specific requests of Connor. He was open to change, but not having to prove himself to her. The therapist emphasized that Megan had to learn to love the real Connor, not her movie star image of a lover.

Megan and Connor had fallen into the destructive pattern of arguing about sex while nude in bed after a negative sexual encounter. Never talk sex while nude in bed after a negative experience. People say things in hurt and anger, especially when they have been drinking. They apologize the next day, but the damage has been done. This adds to alienation and the blame—counter blame dynamic. Megan and Connor realized this had led to the destructive state of their marriage and marital sexuality. Once aware, they committed to being intimate and erotic allies and building a satisfying, secure, and sexual marriage.

The therapist guided them in the rebuilding process. She made the point that sex was not the principal factor in marital satisfaction, but their non-sexual marriage was a major drain. Now marital sexuality energized their bond and reinforced feelings of desire and desirability.

Sexuality contributes 15–20% to a relationship with a focus on sharing pleasure, reinforcing intimacy, and serving as a tension reducer to deal with a shared life and the vicissitudes of life. After Megan and Connor established a satisfying and secure marriage, being sexual with the goal of a planned, wanted child was an aphrodisiac.

Megan and Connor created a relapse prevention plan which included meeting with the therapist for six-month follow-up sessions over two years. If a problem or crisis occurred they would call for a booster session. They had come too far to allow a relapse. Sexuality cannot be taken for granted nor treated with benign neglect. Connor and Megan were committed to a satisfying, secure, and sexual marriage and healthy family.

## The Role of Psychosexual Skill Exercises

In addition to information, guidelines, strategies, techniques, and case studies, this book will include a psychosexual skill exercise in each chapter. The psychosexual skill exercise is intended to make concepts personal and concrete. "Sexually one size never fits all", so not all exercises will be helpful. If an exercise is not right for you, feel free to skip it or engage only the components which are relevant. The exercises are not performances to prove something to you or your partner, but to develop sexual comfort and confidence.

Healthy sexuality involves congruence among attitudes, behavior, and emotions. This begins by confronting old and new sexual myths. Replace myths with personally relevant, scientifically validated sexual awareness and understanding.

## Exercise: Confronting Sexual Myths and Adopting Healthy Sexual Attitudes and Values

This exercise has two phases—first engaging by yourself and then with your partner. This format reinforces a core concept. First, you are responsible for your own sexuality. Second, sex is a team sport, so you learn to be an intimate sexual team.

Confront destructive myths and replace them with personally relevant, scientifically validated awareness. Own your sexual voice. Make personal and concrete the concept that knowledge is power. You owe it to yourself, your partner, and your relationship to accept positive, realistic, scientifically validated information. As well, be aware of your uniqueness as a person and a couple.

The second part of the exercise involves engaging your partner as your intimate and erotic friend. Share the myths which had the most negative impact on you. Tell your partner what he/she can do to help you embrace new understandings and feelings. For example, you believed that the only right way to experience orgasm was through intercourse thrusting and not using additional stimulation. Discuss what each of you now know about the range of normal orgasmic response. Then share your "orgasmic voice"— your preferred way(s) of experiencing orgasm. Accept that your orgasmic pattern is healthy for you as a woman and for couple sexuality. If you are in the one in three category of women who are orgasmic with manual, oral, and/or rubbing stimulation, rather than in intercourse, accept this as a healthy orgasmic response for you. Next, guide your partner about when and how you want to transition from sensual to erotic touch and the type of multiple stimulation which allows you to let go and "come". Most women (and men) find enjoying private erotic fantasies serves as a bridge to high arousal and orgasm. If your orgasmic voice involves multiple stimulation during intercourse, share your preferences and guide him as your intimate and erotic friend in sharing orgasm. The sequence is awareness, verbal requests, and the most crucial factor is enacting your comfort, pleasure, arousal, erotic flow, orgasm pattern.

## Who We are and the Format of this Book

Barry and Emily McCarthy are a husband—wife writing team; this is our 14th co-authored book. When we married in 1966, the male—female double standard was dominant. We were the first in our families to graduate college and were committed to living our lives in a healthier manner than our backgrounds. We wanted to create a life we could be proud of personally and relationally. However, we assumed there would be major differences sexually. We have challenged this assumption and committed to creating a satisfying, secure, and sexual marriage. We are not clones of each other, but approach our sexual bond as partners who affirm desire/pleasure/eroticism/satisfaction.

Writing this book has been an enjoyable challenge. This is our favorite book. We are pro-female, pro-male, pro-couple, and pro-sexual. We promote the 15–20% role of sexuality in individual and couple well-being whether you are 26, 46, or 76. This book has value for women, men, couples, clinicians, and the culture. We confront the harmful effects of the double standard which emphasizes male—female differences and splits intimacy and eroticism. Scientifically, clinically, and personally we advocate for the female—male equity model.

We respect each other's contributions to the writing of this book. Emily's background is in speech communication and her writing and wisdom provides a balanced, humanistic perspective. Barry's background is a professor of psychology and a clinical psychologist with a specialty in couple and sex therapy. This book is written for the public, with grounding in scientifically and clinically validated psychological, biological/medical, and social/relational information to promote healthy sexuality. Knowledge is power. We hope to empower and motivate you to embrace couple sexuality. In his clinical practice, Barry dealt with chronic psychological, relational, and sexual problems. If the couple had the motivation and skills to prevent these problems or dealt with them in the acute phase, their lives would have been so much better. Prevention is the best, cheapest, and most efficacious way to address sexual issues.

We present scientifically and clinically validated sexual information, and provide guidelines, psychosexual skill exercises and case studies (we use composite cases with details altered to protect confidentiality) to make concepts personal and concrete. This is not meant to be read as a textbook; instead each chapter is self-contained. Read chapters which are personally relevant. The material can be read for information and concepts but is best used as an interactive learning medium. Share this with your spouse/partner. Talking and sharing (especially the exercises) make these concepts personal and meaningful. Implement relevant strategies, skills, and coping techniques so that sexuality has a 15–20% positive role in your life and relationship.

This book is in opposition to the heteronormative model which advocates for heterosexual marriage as the only acceptable form of sexuality. We emphasize each person being their "authentic sexual self". This includes sexual orientation (heterosexual, lesbian, bi-sexual, asexual). We affirm healthy sexuality whether you are married, partnered, divorced, single, or widowed. Our message about healthy couple sexuality is relevant whether you are 30, 50, or 80. We emphasize traditional heterosexual married couples, but most of these learnings are applicable to partnered, lesbian, or gay couples.

This is a book of ideas, guidelines, and exercises; it is not a "do it yourself therapy" book. The more information, understandings, and resources, the more likely you will make "wise" sexual decisions. The psychosexual skill exercises help you assess and change attitudes, behaviors, and feelings. Seeking sex, couple, or individual therapy is a wise decision. Appendix A provides information and guidelines on how to choose a sex therapist, couple therapist, or individual therapist.

## Summary

The prevalence and power of sexual myths is astounding. Old myths based on ignorance and repressive attitudes die hard. Conservative people and cultures cling to these myths with the mistaken belief that the old ways, especially based on male—female differences, is good for the culture and prevents sexual drama and problems. The new sex myths are promoted by the internet and media. They are based on a performance approach to sex and erotic perfectionism. The new sex myths are intimidating, filled with promises of the greatest, most liberating sex in the world. The new sex myths cause you to feel inferior and not "good enough" sexually.

Scientific sexology recognizes that sex is multi-causal and multi-dimensional, with large individual, couple, cultural, and value differences. Sexuality honors individuality and diversity. Scientific sexuality recognizes the one—two combination of individual responsibility and being an intimate sexual team. Most couples (married, partnered, lesbian, and a significant percentage of gay male couples) have traditional values regarding prioritizing their relationship and commitment to monogamy. It is crucial that you have a genuine dialogue and agreement about your relationship and the role of sexuality rather than assuming you share the same understandings and values.

A key to healthy sexuality is to recognize that sex is good rather than bad and that sexuality is integral to you as a woman or man. Does sexuality have a positive 15–20% role in your life? The paradox is that sexual conflicts, dysfunction, or avoidance causes more negative impact than the positive role of healthy sexuality.

You owe it to yourself, your partner, and your relationship to confront sex myths, increase sexual knowledge and awareness, and enjoy healthy sexuality for yourself and your intimate relationship.

# 2

# THE NEW SEXUAL MANTRA

Masters and Johnson mistakenly assumed that increased arousal and orgasm was the key to sexual satisfaction. We honor the work of Masters and Johnson, who are the "grandparents" of the sex therapy field. However, they missed the core issue—sexual desire. The new mantra for healthy sexuality is desire/pleasure/eroticism/satisfaction (Foley, Kope & Sugrue, 2012). Of these four dimensions, desire is the most important. Satisfaction is second in importance, with pleasure and eroticism integral to healthy sexuality.

The belief that the essence of sexuality is arousal and orgasm is misleading in two ways. First, it reinforces the performance approach to sex. In truth, the foundation of couple sexuality is giving and receiving pleasure-oriented touch. Pleasure is the essence of sexuality (Byers & Rehman, 2014). Sex is not an individual pass—fail performance test. Second, it reinforces the mistaken belief that desire is contingent on arousal and orgasm.

The new mantra of desire/pleasure/eroticism/satisfaction represents an integrated approach to couple sexuality. Unfortunately, the sex field has multiple splits—between men and women, between foreplay and intercourse, between intimacy and eroticism, between orgasm and pleasure, between bonding and illicitness. Healthy sexuality involves congruence among sexual attitudes, behavior, and emotions. It honors sexual similarities between women and men. Both partners value intimacy and eroticism. You value affectionate, sensual, playful, and erotic touch in addition to intercourse. Accept the multiple roles, meanings, and outcomes of sexuality rather than sex as a competition with a winner and a loser. Value mutual, synchronous sexual encounters as well as asynchronous experiences (better for one partner than the other) (Metz, Epstein & McCarthy, 2017).

The new mantra recognizes that couple sexuality is multi-causal, multi-dimensional with large individual, couple, cultural, and value differences. Sex is not an individual pass—fail performance test. Sexuality is an integration of attitudes, behavior, and feelings focused on pleasure-oriented touching. We advocate for arousal, intercourse, and orgasm, but when that is the performance goal it undermines desire and satisfaction. You can experience desire without functional sex. You can enjoy sexual pleasure without it leading to arousal. You can enjoy eroticism without intercourse. You can feel sexually satisfied without orgasm.

Accept the complexity of couple sexuality rather than viewing sex as an individual pass—fail performance test. Each dimension of the new sexual mantra has value, but is best when integrated and valued by both partners. Acceptance and integration promotes sexuality, splitting subverts sexuality.

## Understanding Each Dimension of the Sexual Mantra

Desire/pleasure/eroticism/satisfaction is valued for each dimension, and the whole is more than the component parts. Let us explore each dimension.

The most important dimension is desire. Psychologically, the key for desire is positive anticipation, feeling you deserve sexual pleasure, freedom and choice regarding sexual scenarios and techniques, and the unpredictability of the sexual experience. Psychologically, what subverts desire is a performance orientation, anger and coercion, and predictable, mechanical intercourse. Bio-medically, desire is promoted by a healthy body, good behavioral health habits—especially sleep, accepting changes with aging (including being sexual in your 60s, 70s, and 80s), and maintaining a self-accepting body image. Bio-medically what subverts desire is side-effects of medication, allowing illness and disability to control sexual self-esteem, poor behavioral habits—especially smoking, drinking, and drug abuse. Socially/relationally, what promotes desire is the partner being your intimate and erotic ally and adopting positive, realistic sexual expectations based on the Good Enough Sex (GES) model. Socially/relationally what subverts sexual desire are couple power struggles, splitting intimacy and eroticism, and perfectionist erotic expectations (McCarthy, 2015).

Desire is facilitated by receptivity and responsivity to giving and receiving pleasure-oriented touching. In terms of subjective arousal, pleasuring involves sensations/feelings in the 1–5 range (0 is neutral and 10 is orgasm). Non-demand pleasuring includes affectionate, sensual, and playful touch. Pleasure is the foundation for sexual arousal and orgasm. Pleasurable touch can evolve into erotic stimulation. The crucial concept is that pleasure has value whether or not it transitions to arousal. Pleasurable touch (both giving and receiving) reinforces attachment and bonding. Rather than narrowly defining "sex=intercourse", sexuality is a couple process centered on sharing pleasure.

Eroticism is the most contentious dimension of the new mantra. The core of eroticism is intense sexual feelings and sensations. In terms of subjective arousal, eroticism involves 6–10 sensations and feelings. Eroticism usually involves intercourse and orgasm, but you can enjoy eroticism without intercourse. Eroticism includes manual, oral, rubbing, and vibrator stimulation in addition to intercourse.

Unfortunately, people associate eroticism with pornography, out of control sex, breaking boundaries, lust and drama, and male domination. Integrated eroticism is a fundamental dimension of the desire/pleasure/eroticism/satisfaction mantra. Eroticism is healthy for the man, woman, and couple. Eroticism is not hyper masculine or driven by porn. Eroticism is an integral couple dimension. Most scenarios involve partner interaction arousal/eroticism which features each partner's arousal enhancing the other's. It is an erotic dance. The second most common eroticism/arousal scenario is self-entrancement arousal. This involves taking turns, with one partner the giver and the other the receiver. The receiving partner's responsivity enhances your sexual experience. The third eroticism/arousal style is role enactment arousal, which involves outside resources to provide an erotic charge. This can include watching X-rated videos, using sex toys, playing out an erotic fantasy, using blind-folds or handcuffs, or doing a strip-tease. This is the type of eroticism featured on the internet and in the media, but is the least used. The key feature in eroticism is celebrating intense sensations and feelings. Eroticism involves mystery and creativity, encourages risk-taking and experimentation, is unpredictable, and is not "socially acceptable".

Satisfaction certainly includes orgasm, but satisfaction is more than orgasm. Satisfaction involves feeling good about yourself as a sexual person and energized as a sexual couple. Orgasm as a pass—fail test interferes with satisfaction. A valuable learning is to identify a sexual encounter where the non-orgasmic partner feels more satisfied than the orgasmic partner. A major turn-off for women is when the first thing the man says is "Did you come?"

Feeling satisfied personally and as a couple is more important than sex function. The best sex is mutual and synchronous—both partners experience desire/pleasure/eroticism/satisfaction. Accept that most sexual encounters are positive yet asynchronous. Asynchronous means that the experience was better for one partner than the other. For couples under 40, sex is often better for the man than the woman. For couples over 60, sex is often better for the woman. This gender transition is a challenge for the couple.

The key for sexual satisfaction is positive, realistic expectations. Expecting each sexual encounter to be mutual and wonderful sets you up for disappointment and frustration. By its nature couple sexuality is variable and flexible. Couple sexuality has many roles, meanings, and outcomes. Good Enough Sex (GES) is motivating and empowering. Demanding perfect sex performance and that all sex be mutual subverts satisfaction. Accepting both synchronous and asynchronous sexual experiences promotes satisfaction.

A crucial concept is that among happy, sexually functional couples 5–15% of sexual experiences are dissatisfying or dysfunctional (Frank, Anderson & Rubinstein, 1978). This is almost never discussed in the media. The promise is that with love and communication, or being erotic and free, that all sex will be great. The sign of a healthy couple is turning toward each other whether the sexual experience was "dynamite", very good, good, okay, mediocre, dissatisfying, or dysfunctional. You are an intimate sexual team in good and bad times. Being intimate and erotic allies promotes satisfaction even when the sexual encounter is disappointing, frustrating, or dysfunctional. Satisfaction involves both emotional and sexual components.

Ideally, the marriage (partnered relationship) is satisfying, secure, and sexual. Sexuality is not the major factor. Sexuality is a 15–20% factor which reinforces feelings of desire and desirability and energizes your couple bond. The paradox is that dysfunctional, conflictual, and especially avoidant sexuality has a powerful negative role. Sexual problems demoralize the person and threaten relational stability. Sadly, sexual problems are more impactful than the positive role of healthy couple sexuality.

You deserve sexuality to be positive in your life and relationship. Sexuality nurtures your bond, reinforces intimacy and attachment, and is a tension reducer to deal with life stresses, including sharing life with your partner. For those who want children the traditional biological function of procreation enhances desire. Having a child is not a mandate, it is a decision. Couples who decide not to have children have a better sexual relationship. Children are a decision and commitment.

A paradox is that sex cannot save a marriage, but sexual problems, conflicts, and avoidance can destroy a marriage (Meana, 2010). Adopting the mantra of desire/pleasure/eroticism/satisfaction promotes couple sexuality.

### Dana and Trevor

Like most couples, Dana and Trevor began as a romantic love/passionate sex/idealized couple (limerance phase). Limerance is a very special experience, but fragile and time limited (six months to two years). Like so many couples, Dana and Trevor did not make the transition to develop a couple sexual style which integrated desire/pleasure/ eroticism/satisfaction. Eleven years into their marriage they still experience wonderful sexual encounters, especially on vacation, but most of the time sex is routine, typically occurring on a weekend night after the children are asleep. Touching always ends with intercourse. Trevor is orgasmic inside Dana, and then he manually stimulates her to orgasm. Dana enjoys orgasm, but often it feels like work and sometimes she fakes orgasm to please Trevor and end the encounter. Trevor tries very hard to satisfy Dana, but this increases her self-consciousness. Sex feels more like a work task than a shared pleasure. Nevertheless, Trevor and Dana valued marital sex.

The vulnerability of routine couple sex is that it lacks special feelings and does not energize your bond. Although it is normal and healthy for each partner to occasionally masturbate, masturbation was a sensitive issue for Dana and Trevor, but for very different reasons. Desire/pleasure/eroticism were higher for Dana in masturbation than couple sex, although she felt more satisfied after couple sex. Dana never spoke about this with Trevor. When female friends joked about masturbation, they said women know their bodies—that's why it's easier. Trevor masturbated two to four times a week. He resented masturbation because he saw it as a poor substitute for "real sex".

Trevor and Dana would have benefitted by addressing sexuality concerns early in their marriage. It usually takes a crisis or major negative experience to start the professional intervention process. The cue was a couple that Trevor and Dana were friends with who separated over a sexual power struggle. The wife found the husband was spending almost $400 a month on internet sex sites and strip clubs. She told Dana that the husband was a "sex addict". The husband told Trevor the real problem was that his wife would rather play bridge than have sex.

Observing this power struggle was a wake-up call for Dana and Trevor. They did not want this drama to subvert their lives and marriage. They realized that sex had become a source of misunderstanding and frustration. They were aware that sex cannot solve problems. However, sexuality was no longer a positive resource in their marriage.

The couple therapist suggested a comprehensive approach to addressing relational and sexual issues. Relationally, Dana and Trevor needed to reinforce respect, trust, and emotional commitment. They adopted a Best Friend relational style. However, the Best Friend sexual style was not the right fit. Dana had hoped that with increased communication and cuddling she would feel greater desire. Cuddling is good for emotional intimacy, but too much cuddling can subvert desire because you lose erotic anticipation. Dana had fallen into the traditional trap of losing her "sexual voice", feeling sex was Trevor's domain. When you view sex as a task, and especially when you split intimacy and eroticism, it robs the sexual experience of shared meaning and bonding. This is what happened with Trevor and Dana. It was not intentional, but it did subvert Dana's desire.

The therapist asked when in their relationship desire/pleasure/eroticism/satisfaction was best. They agreed it was the limerance phase and cherished special memories of those two years. Trevor valued intercourse and orgasm but was disappointed that Dana did not value their sexual relationship. Like the majority of men, Trevor believed the key was Dana achieving orgasm during intercourse. He hoped if intercourse lasted at least ten minutes she would orgasm. He had never discussed this with Dana. Sadly, a very common pattern.

The therapist was empathic and respectful of both Dana and Trevor, but confrontative that their unspoken assumptions were wrong and self-defeating.

The key is desire and pleasure, not intercourse and orgasm. Orgasm is a positive, integral part of female sexuality. However, few women have the same orgasmic response as men. The vast majority of men have a single orgasm during intercourse without needing additional erotic stimulation. Only about one in seven women have that orgasmic pattern. If you are in that group enjoy your orgasmic voice, but don't label the majority of women as having an orgasm dysfunction. Approximately two in three women do experience orgasm during intercourse. The key is multiple stimulation during intercourse, especially clitoral stimulation and freedom to enjoy her private erotic fantasies. It is crucial to understand that one in three women are never or almost never orgasmic during intercourse. For these women their orgasmic pattern is with manual, oral, rubbing, or vibrator stimulation. This is a normal, healthy variation of female sexuality, not a dysfunction. This was a motivating and empowering insight for Dana as well as useful information for Trevor.

The foundation for individual and couple sexuality is acceptance. Dana's pleasure/eroticism pattern involved manual and oral stimulation to orgasm during pleasuring rather than during intercourse. For Dana and Trevor (and many, if not most, couples) sexuality is more satisfying if she is orgasmic first and then Trevor orgasms during intercourse. It is easiest to change attitudes (sexual knowledge) and behavior (sexual scenarios) than accept changes in sexual feelings. Once they incorporated Dana being orgasmic with manual and/or oral stimulation and then Trevor let go and orgasmed during intercourse, sexual confidence grew. Dana owning her desire/pleasure/eroticism/satisfaction pattern made it easier for Trevor to accept their new couple sexuality. Instead of "working to achieve orgasm" her pleasure/eroticism flow naturally transitioned to orgasm.

Dana embraced her orgasmic pattern as healthy for her, though different than Trevor's. When pleasure/eroticism did not flow, she didn't work against her body to achieve (or fake) orgasm to placate Trevor. She was comfortable saying this was a positive experience (subjective arousal of 4 or 7), but wasn't going to be an orgasmic encounter.

Dana and Trevor read and dialogued about satisfaction being more than orgasm. The key was the actual experience where Dana felt a pleasurable 5, told Trevor she felt good and wanted him inside her, and he ejaculated after four minutes of thrusting. As they lay together, Trevor said he'd enjoyed the sex. She acknowledged that and told him that this was more positive than past experiences where she felt pressure to have an orgasm. She felt better about herself as a sexual woman. Dana assured Trevor she valued orgasm (and no longer felt she had to fake orgasm). Sharing pleasure allowed her to feel bonded with Trevor. Dana's variable, flexible approach to couple sexuality and orgasm was right for her. This included orgasmic experiences where she let go and felt lost in erotic sensations and feelings.

Attitudinally, behaviorally, and emotionally Dana and Trevor were speaking the language of desire/pleasure/eroticism/satisfaction. This included accepting that they were not sexual clones. Each had a sexual voice and were intimate and erotic allies. Trevor accepted that Dana's sexual response was more variable and flexible than his, but not inferior.

Dana claimed her erotic voice as part of her sexuality. The core learning was that Trevor was her sexual friend. Rather than pressuring her to have orgasms like him, Trevor embraced the variability of Dana's orgasm and satisfaction pattern. Couple sexuality is a one—two process of accepting your authentic sexual self and being an intimate sexual team.

## Shared Meaning for Couple Sexuality

The desire/pleasure/eroticism/satisfaction mantra emphasizes two concepts. First, a common sexual language which challenges traditional gender and sex splits. Second, the need to recognize the potential roles, meanings, and outcomes of couple sexuality rather than thinking of sex as a routine, predictable intercourse performance. Sexuality thrives when each partner's sexual voice is honored and the couple recognize that they are not clones. Accept the range of your sexual experiences rather than demanding that each encounter be mutual and perfect. Sometimes one partner is desirous and forcefully initiates. Much of the time the sexual experience involves intercourse, but not always. Intercourse is not a pass—fail test.

Seldom are both partners equally desirous before a sexual encounter. Openness and receptivity to touch and feeling you deserve pleasure are important bridges to desire. You cannot force or demand desire. You can enjoy your partner's initiation and desire, especially when you are free to say "yes", "no", or suggest an alternative way to connect. The man wants to feel that his sexual interest is welcomed and the woman to feel desired and desirable. Asynchronous desire is normal and healthy as long as the lower desire partner does not feel pressured or coerced.

The essence of couple sexuality is giving and receiving pleasure-oriented touching. Pleasure and consent is the foundation. Most couples prefer mutual giving and receiving while others prefer taking turns. Affectionate, sensual, and playful touch is the milieu for pleasure. For women, a key is being active in the pleasuring process rather than passive during "foreplay". For men, a key is to enjoy pleasuring for himself rather than "working" to arouse his partner. His erection is a natural response to pleasure rather than pressure for her to "catch up" or a demand for intercourse. Losing the pleasure focus and allowing performance pressure subverts couple sexuality. This is true for both partners.

A common trap is the belief that pleasure must lead to intercourse and orgasm. Pleasure can be a bridge to arousal, intercourse, and orgasm, but pleasure is valuable for itself. Enjoying pleasurable touch allows desire to "simmer", leading to better quality and more sex. The best example of this distinction is his erection. A pleasure-orientation facilitates the woman welcoming his erection. The performance-orientation sees his erection as a demand, and if you don't want to be sexual at that time, his erection is a source of conflict.

Eroticism is integral to the desire/pleasure/eroticism/satisfaction mantra. Conflicts over eroticism disrupt sexual desire. Is eroticism integrated into couple sexuality, or does it split sexuality? Eroticism is a bridge for intercourse and orgasm; intercourse is the natural continuation of the pleasuring/eroticism process. However, when eroticism is a performance test to impress your partner or prove yourself, it undercuts desire. Integrate eroticism into your couple sexual style. This honors both your erotic voice and your partner's erotic voice. Whether your erotic/arousal style is partner interaction, self-entrancement, or role enactment, be sure it enhances couple sexuality.

The major mistake people make about eroticism is to focus on the demand for intense sexual response when your level of subjective pleasure is low. There is nothing more anti-erotic than self-consciousness. Working at eroticism using manual or oral stimulation at low levels of arousal subverts sexual response. If subjective arousal is 6 or 7, genital stimulation will build erotic flow. If subjective arousal is 2 or 3, genital stimulation raises performance anxiety and decreases arousal. Eroticism is about intense sensations/feelings. Go with the pleasuring/eroticism flow. Don't work against your body. Embrace integrated eroticism.

Satisfaction is the second most important dimension and reflects the importance of individual and couple factors. Satisfaction is about acceptance, not contingent on performance. The best sexuality is mutual and synchronous. However, most sexual encounters are asynchronous. The sexual encounter is better for one partner, although not at the expense of the other. Ideally, you feel bonded and energized after a sexual encounter. At a minimum, you feel better after sex. Orgasm is valued, but not as a performance measure. For both partners, satisfaction is more important than orgasm.

### Exercise: Enhancing Desire/Pleasure/Eroticism/Satisfaction

This exercise recognizes that the whole is more important than a component part and that each dimension is valuable for itself. The new mantra provides you with a language and set of strategies to enhance sexuality. It allows each partner to develop your sexual voice and as an intimate team to accept the multiple roles, meanings, and outcomes of couple sexuality.

Let's start with the most important dimension—desire. This exercise recognizes a paradox—unless you have the power to say "no" to sex you do not have the freedom to own your sexual desire. This is equally true for men and women—do not be controlled by traditional gender expectations. Be clear and specific with your partner (and yourself) about a non-verbal signal or a verbal phrase that says you do not consent to a sexual encounter or a specific scenario. Do you trust your partner will honor your veto rather than cajole or force their sexual initiative? The power of "no" builds the foundation for strong, resilient sexual desire.

You cannot will or force desire. For women, men, and couples desire comes and goes. Desire is based on positive anticipation, sense of deserving pleasure, freedom and choice, and unpredictable sexual scenarios. A common type of desire is "responsive sexual desire". This means it is okay to start at neutral. When you are receptive and responsive to giving and receiving pleasure-oriented touch and open to your feelings as well as your partner's feelings, you experience 1–4 subjective pleasure. Responsive desire is a reaction to physical and emotional connection; different than spontaneous desire. Spontaneous desire is the traditional male pattern while responsive desire is more common for women. As men age, responsive desire becomes more common. The crucial factor is to identify your desire turn-ons and your desire turn-offs. Share these with your partner. A motivating concept is "bridges to desire". What mood, situation, activity, partner behavior, types of touch, fantasy, sexual cues make sex inviting for you?

Although everyone loves spontaneous sex, the reality for the great majority of couples is that sexual encounters are planned or semi-planned (although not rigidly). If all sex had to be spontaneous, there would be low sex frequency. Awareness of what invites a sexual encounter is crucial. Share between two and five of your favorite bridges to desire, but keep one to three private (for special occasions).

We advocate for a regular rhythm of touching and intercourse. Accept sexual pleasure as part of your life and relationship. Sex is not awkward nor an event to prove something.

Let's focus on the second dimension—pleasure. Most couples only have two gears of touch—affection and intercourse. This dramatically limits pleasure. Ideally, both partners value affectionate, sensual, playful, erotic, and intercourse touch. Intercourse is the natural continuation of the pleasure/eroticism process, not a performance test. Most couples fall into the "sex=intercourse" trap. This results in less touching and less intercourse. Couples who embrace a pleasure-oriented approach to touching experience more touching and more intercourse.

Like desire, pleasure comes and goes. Often one partner finds a scenario or technique more pleasurable than the other. This is normal and healthy. What is unhealthy is feeling pressure to feel something you're not feeling or demand mutual levels of pleasure.

Do not touch with the goal of arousing your partner or causing an orgasm. Touch and be touched in ways which are pleasurable for you. Your responsivity is pleasurable for your partner. It's like a dance—a receptive, responsive partner is the major aphrodisiac.

The next part of this exercise focuses on eroticism, the most misunderstood and contentious dimension. The trap is splitting eroticism or the meaning of sex by gender. In this exercise both partners own their "erotic voice". Eroticism is not an aggressive, lustful, male-dominate concept. Eroticism is about intense sensations and emotions—applicable to women and men. What promotes eroticism for you? Does partner interaction arousal/eroticism allow you to go from subjective arousal to erotic flow? Is self-entrancement arousal/eroticism a turn-on for you? Is role-enactment arousal/eroticism inviting for you? What erotic scenarios are most exciting? If your partner's scenarios are a turn-off, do you have the courage to say "no" and use your sexual veto? This frees you to enjoy erotic scenarios and techniques. Remember, unless subjective pleasure/arousal is 4 or 5 eroticism is not inviting.

The satisfaction dimension is particularly important. Satisfaction is subjective, not an objective measure based on function. What allows you to feel good about yourself as a sexual person and energized as a sexual couple? Vital, satisfying couple sexuality is more than functional sex and more than orgasm (although both are important). Satisfaction is about expectations and meanings. The Good Enough Sex (GES) concept acknowledges that sometimes sex is wonderful for both partners, sometimes the sexual experience is better for one than the other (asynchronous sex), sometimes the sexual encounter is positive and mutual (synchronous sex), sometimes it is about intimate connection for one partner while for the other orgasm is key, sometimes sex is mediocre, and in 5–15% of encounters sex is dissatisfying or dysfunctional. Having at least one (and usually more) negative sexual experiences a year is an almost universal experience. A key for satisfaction is to accept this range of sexual experiences and turn toward each other as intimate and erotic friends whether the sex was great, good, okay, or dysfunctional.

What can you do to enhance satisfaction so that couple sexuality has a 15–20% role in your life and relationship? Can you embrace

GES? Can you enjoy both synchronous and asynchronous sexuality? Can you celebrate great sex and turn toward each other even when the sex is mediocre or dysfunctional? Can you enjoy orgasm while feeling satisfied if you are not orgasmic? Can you accept that the essence of satisfying sexuality is sharing pleasure?

All four dimensions—desire/pleasure/eroticism/satisfaction—are important. Yet, the whole is more than each component. Celebrate this integrated approach to couple sexuality.

## Summary

The new mantra of desire/pleasure/eroticism/satisfaction is a breakthrough for couple sexuality. Rather than splitting by gender or arguing about the role of sex, this mantra provides a coherent, comprehensive approach for the woman, man, and couple. It recognizes the multiple roles, meanings, and outcomes of couple sexuality. Emphasizing the core role of desire and satisfaction challenges the media overemphasis on arousal, intercourse, and orgasm. Couple sexuality is more important than any dimension. Value desire/pleasure/eroticism/satisfaction for you and your relationship.

# 3

# PSYCHOBIOSOCIAL MODEL FOR UNDERSTANDING AND CHANGE

A helpful understanding from the 50 years of sex therapy research and clinical findings is how complex sexuality is, especially couple sexuality. Contrary to media ads for Viagra and testosterone, a comprehensive psychobiosocial approach to understanding, assessment, and treatment is crucial in resolving sexual problems (McCarthy & Wald, 2017). Even more important, a comprehensive couple approach promotes healthy sexuality. The proper term is "biopsychosocial", but because psychological factors are crucial, especially for sexual desire and satisfaction, we encourage you to utilize the psychobiosocial approach in your life and relationship.

You know something is "pop sex" when the answer is simple, fits everyone, works perfectly, and promises the intervention (whether bio-medical, psychological, or relational) cures all problems and works for all couples. In the psychobiosocial approach, you explore psychological, bio-medical, and social/relational factors and tailor change strategies to your problem. In terms of change, one size never fits all and there are no guarantees. However, the chance of successful resolution is much higher if you consider all relevant factors and have a comprehensive approach to the complexity of the sexual problems as well as positive, realistic expectations of change rather than "perfectionistic" or "magical" expectations (McCarthy & Metz, 2008).

Unfortunately, both in the public and professional cultures there is a powerful trend to "medicalize" sexuality. The first line intervention is to consult a physician, especially for erectile dysfunction (ED). Viagra or testosterone are the most used interventions. Sex is embodied and understanding the role of vascular, neurological, and hormonal factors is crucial, this simplistic medical approach usually backfires. This demoralizes the man and the couple. Although a pro-erection medication can be a valuable therapeutic resource, the sad truth is that Viagra has caused more non-sexual relationships than anything else in history (Metz & McCarthy, 2004). Everyone (man, woman, child), has seen the Viagra commercials which promise a return to the totally predictable erections of your youth. Almost no man gets the results promised by the ads. This does not mean he's a "Viagra failure". What it means is that you (and your partner) would benefit from a comprehensive couple psychobiosocial assessment and treatment. Medication as a stand-alone intervention is seldom successful in the long term (Leiblum, 2002).

The most common psychological factors in ED include anticipatory anxiety, anger, depression, a secret arousal pattern, and shame about a sexual trauma history. Common bio-medical factors include vascular disease, neurological problems, severe testosterone deficit, smoking, alcohol or drug abuse, uncontrolled diabetes, side-effects of chemotherapy, and fatigue caused by sleep apnea. Common social/relational factors include an alienated relationship, de-eroticizing the partner, a shameful approach to sex, not valuing relationship sex, power struggles over intercourse frequency, conflicts about sexual betrayal, and disagreements about contraception.

The crucial issue is whether ED is viewed as a couple problem or the man's problem. Generally, approaching sexual problems as a couple issue leads to success, especially for the long term. When using a pro-erection medication, how do you integrate this in your couple sexual style of intimacy, pleasuring, and eroticism? The major reason men fail with Viagra is that as soon as he becomes erect, he rushes to intercourse because he fears losing his erection. A crucial technique is to transition to intercourse when your subjective arousal is high. Your partner can guide intromission so you stay with the arousal/erotic flow process rather than be distracted by performance anxiety. Some couples find Viagra a helpful intervention because it provides a one to four-hour window to initiate sex. This is particularly valuable for procrastinators and avoiders. Other couples prefer

Cialis since it gives them a wide window of opportunity of when to be sexual (30 minutes to 30 hours). This allows greater freedom—sexual initiation feels "natural".

The principal factor favoring the couple psychobiosocial approach involves sexual expectations. Rather than demanding perfect performance and viewing intercourse as an individual pass—fail test, the psychobiosocial model embraces Good Enough Sex (GES) which emphasizes sexuality as a couple process (Metz & McCarthy, 2012). The core of sexuality is giving and receiving pleasure. Men learn erection and intercourse as a totally predictable, autonomous function. After you have a "sensitizing" experience (don't have an erection sufficient for intercourse), you seldom return to autonomous sex function. You become a better lover, but not a perfect performer. GES is more easily accepted by women because it's congruent with your lived sexual experience. GES is difficult for men, male physicians, and drug companies to accept. Yet, GES is the key to being sexual in your 50s, 60s, 70s, and 80s. Another example of the superiority of the psychobiosocial model in comparison to the biomedical model.

## Individual Performance vs. Couple Sexual Pleasure

A core issue is whether you view sex as an individual performance or a couple process of sharing pleasure. The original Masters and Johnson model emphasized individual sex function and dysfunction, although their treatment approach was couple therapy. In the past 50 years, it has become clear that the couple model of sexuality as sharing pleasure promotes desire and satisfaction. Unfortunately, this has not translated to the medical profession nor to the media. Thus, people remain trapped in the individual sex dysfunction model. Sex is viewed as a pass—fail performance test emphasizing arousal, intercourse, and orgasm. Although we advocate for arousal, intercourse, and orgasm, this misses the core issue. The new sexual mantra is desire/pleasure/eroticism/satisfaction. Desire is the most important dimension. Desire is not a performance; desire is facilitated by a couple approach to giving and receiving pleasure-oriented touching. An individual sex performance orientation ultimately subverts desire and couple sexuality.

Does "sex=intercourse"? That is the usual approach, but this subverts sexual acceptance. Intercourse is integral to sexuality, but sexuality is much more than intercourse. Sexuality involves sensual, playful, and erotic scenarios in addition to intercourse. "Intercourse=sex" is rigid and limited. Healthy sexuality focuses on sharing pleasure. GES emphasizes the couple process of desire/pleasure/eroticism/satisfaction. When dealing with a sexual dysfunction (whether male or female), the emphasis is a broad-based psychobiosocial approach to promote desire and pleasure. Emphasizing couple sexuality rather than individual performance motivates both. Couple sexuality can have a range of roles, meanings, and outcomes. This empowering insight is in contrast to sex as an individual performance.

Psychological factors are more important than bio-medical factors. An example is a couple dealing with the woman's breast cancer. Surviving the cancer is the primary agenda. The partner's support is crucial. You deal with the illness as well as the side-effects of radiation or chemotherapy. Yet, you are more than the cancer. Engaging in touching—whether affectionate, sensual, playful, erotic, or intercourse—promotes your quality of life. The key psychological factor is whether you feel you deserve touching and pleasure as you deal with cancer. Trust that your partner will honor your veto of types of touch which are uncomfortable. For example, most women feel that since the diagnosis breast stimulation is no longer enjoyable. When fatigued you do not welcome sexual touch, although you enjoy a back massage. Bio-medical and social/relational factors are integral to sexuality, but the key factor is psychological. Couple sexuality is much more than individual sex function/dysfunction.

## Dialogue about the Psychobiosocial Model of Sexuality and Change

This book encourages using knowledge and awareness to enhance couple sexuality. This isn't an academic perspective; it has relevance to you, your partner, and your sexual relationship. We suggest dialoguing about sexuality.

What sexual problems have you faced and how have you attempted to change them? Did you learn nothing or learn that sex is primarily bio-medical? We bet you didn't learn the psychobiosocial model of sex. Discuss what aspects of your learning were helpful as well as aspects that were misleading or harmful. What do you need to understand and implement so that the psychobiosocial model promotes your sexuality?

Psychologically for you, what facilitates and what subverts sexuality? Is sex a good or bad thing in your life? People are aware of the negative or traumatic aspects of sexuality (unwanted pregnancy, STI/HIV, sexual abuse and trauma, rape and sexual harassment, being exhibited to or peeped on, the object of sexual jokes or hassles, feeling intimidated or coerced sexually, feeling guilty about masturbation or sexual fantasies). There are negative sexual experiences in everyone's life. Remaining aware that the essence of sexuality is pleasure and consent puts these negatives in perspective. A second dimension is acceptance that sexuality is integral for you as a female or male. This is the foundation of equitable gender roles. Healthy sexuality is good for the woman, man, couple, and culture. An important factor is the motivation and ability to make "wise" sexual decisions. Rather than sex being controlled by dramatic emotions or physical urges, the wise decision is to act in your best interest in the context of a healthy relationship and congruent with your values. Sex is not about acting impulsively when under the influence of alcohol or drugs. Sexuality is about self-awareness and self-acceptance. Your attitudes, behaviors, and emotions are positive and congruent. You deserve sexual pleasure.

Bio-medically, you own your body and express sexuality in a healthy manner. This means a commitment to using effective contraception (usually a long-acting reversible contraceptive such as an IUD or birth control pills), practicing safe sex, and not needing drugs, alcohol, illicitness, or drama to enjoy sex. It means confronting and changing self-defeating behavioral health patterns of poor sleep, lack of exercise, smoking or alcohol abuse, obesity or an eating disorder, or only feeling sexual when high. For individuals and couples dealing with illness or disability (whether heart disease or paraplegia), sexual health involves being an active patient who accepts the illness or disability, but does not allow it to define them or their sexuality. There is no illness or disability which stops sexuality, especially not sexual desire. Illness alters sexual function, but you and your partner remain open to desire/pleasure/eroticism/satisfaction. The bio-medical challenge is to accept the "new normal" and create a couple sexuality that accepts the physical changes while continuing to share pleasure as intimate and erotic allies. You are a sexual team who accept and enjoy each other's bodies. You incorporate the "new normal" of physical loss which includes a mourning process and a change of expectations of physical response. No one welcomes an illness or disability. View this as a psychological, relational, and sexual challenge to accept the "new normal" and value sexual pleasure.

Social/relational factors are crucial in the psychobiosocial model. Few cultures are unequivocally pro-sexual. Sadly, the US is an ambivalent sexual culture. Although sex is featured in the media and sexual jokes are pervasive, discussing personally relevant, scientifically validated sexual information is rare. There is a plethora of self-help materials on marriage and relationships. Some are harmful while most are irrelevant or unrealistic. There is little scientifically validated material on healthy couple sexuality.

Social/relational factors are crucial in the psychobiosocial model. The healthiest relationship is satisfying, secure, and sexual. Satisfying is the most important dimension. Satisfying is totally different than an idealized relationship based around romantic love. Satisfying involves your relationship being based on a positive influence model and your ability to deal with differences and conflicts. Contrary to the overpromise of "pop psych", scientific evidence indicates that only 30% of problems are resolvable, 50–60% are modifiable, and even in the best marriages 10–20% of problems need to be accepted and coped with. Being in a healthy relationship brings out the best in you as a person. You feel respected and loved with your strengths and vulnerabilities.

The second most important dimension is a secure relationship. You depend on your partner in good and bad times. Your partner "has your back". People feel trapped in unhealthy relationships (mediocre or unsatisfying). In healthy, secure relationship you value the genuineness, attachment, and predictability of your relationship.

## UNDERSTANDING AND CHANGE

What is the role of intimacy, pleasure, and eroticism? Are all three dimensions valued and integrated in your relationship or do you adhere to the tradition of intimacy being the woman's domain and eroticism the man's domain? What is the role of contraception and children in your approach to sexuality? Do you have a clear agreement about monogamy vs. consensual non-monogamy or do you assume but not discuss? When you have a sexual problem or conflict do you avoid, engage in blame—counter blame, or try to resolve the problem? Social/relational dimensions are crucial in the psychobiosocial model.

## Connor and Miranda

As they prepared for their middle years second marriage, Connor (age 44) had been divorced for two years while 42-year-old Miranda had been a widow for eight years. They are optimistic and hopeful about their marriage. They are aware of the vulnerabilities and challenges of a second marriage and blended family. Connor is a 50–50 co-parent for his 8-year-old son and Miranda has an 11-year-old daughter and 9-year-old son. Miranda was positive with the children about their deceased father, but felt she had always been the primary parent. She realizes that blended families have unique strengths and vulnerabilities and wants their 5-person family to meet the challenges and thrive. Connor and Miranda want to be actively involved parents while recognizing that the core bond in the family is their couple bond. A strong, functional marriage is the foundation of being a parental team. This is a major contribution to the growth and development of children.

Psychologically, a major challenge for Connor is that he never felt good enough as a person, father, worker, or spouse. The divorce had been very hard on his self-esteem. Although he and his ex-wife are cooperative co-parents, she is personally antagonistic toward Connor. She blamed him for the failure of the marriage and insists he needs to attend more to his son and less to the step-children. These attacks are destructive for his already vulnerable self-esteem. Connor had not learned a crucial lesson—you need the support of people who have your best interest in mind. Seldom does this include the ex-spouse. Maintaining a functional co-parenting relationship is a strength. However, he needs to stay away from emotional, relational, and sexual issues with the ex-spouse. He does not want the ex-spouse to have influence on him other than co-parenting. Even more important is to build his self-esteem and utilize social supports, especially Miranda. Miranda's father (a social worker) encouraged Connor to enter individual therapy to address self-esteem issues. The therapist utilizes a cognitive-behavioral approach which challenges his negative self-cognitions. For example, Connor is well-respected in his profession and earns an excellent salary (although not as much as his entrepreneurial ex-brother-in-law). However, Connor does not acknowledge his "good-enough" professional and monetary life. In the same manner, Connor is an active, nurturing parent with all three children, including coaching softball and soccer teams.

The psychological challenges are different for Miranda. The widow role made her feel like a fraud. Miranda had not valued her first marriage. She is satisfied with her marriage to Connor. However, she felt this was not "socially acceptable". Her parents encouraged Miranda to be open and honest with them, close friends, and Connor. A great advantage of close relationships is that people accept you for who you really are. Another challenge for Miranda is to accept that she is a better mother to her biological children than her step-son. Rather than pretending everyone was equal, Miranda adopted a "favorite aunt" role with Connor's son and is pleased that her children accept their step-brother. Miranda realizes (as does Connor) that everyone has strengths and vulnerabilities. The key with vulnerabilities is to accept them, modify if possible, but not allow self-esteem to be controlled by your vulnerabilities.

Bio-medically, emphasize emotional and physical health and primary prevention while recognizing and dealing with health problems. An issue with Miranda is poor sleep patterns, specifically insomnia. The issue for Connor is depression.

In dealing with bio-medical problems, be active. Don't expect the doctor or medication to resolve everything. Medication as a stand-alone intervention is seldom enough. You need to change attitudes, behavior, and health patterns. Rather than a total "cure", successfully managing the health problem is usually the best strategy. Miranda's sleep problems are a good example. Her internist referred her to a sleep clinic where she kept a detailed sleep diary for two weeks. Among suggested interventions was to stop one medication, replace a second medication with one which has less side-effects, stop screen time (computer, TV, cell phone, iPad) an hour before going to sleep, no exercise 90 minutes before sleep, and have yogurt with fruit before bed. In addition, Miranda learned to use mindfulness and pleasant dream themes to facilitate quality sleep. Historically, Connor and Miranda had sex in bed late at night. They agreed to cuddle for relaxation and sensual touch, but not to be sexual before sleep. Probably the most effective intervention for Miranda was going for a walk or bike ride with Connor in the early evening to discuss critical issues so that she did not worry and agitate before bed.

Historically, when Connor was going through his divorce the internist prescribed a course of anti-depressant medication that Connor automatically renewed over the years. This reinforced his self-image as a depressed person. The therapist asked Connor to record feelings before and after taking the medication as well as any sexual side-effects, especially affecting desire and orgasm. Connor was aware of a mild lessening of desire and sensations but enhanced ejaculatory control. The therapist encouraged a consultation with a psychopharmacologist who recommended switching to a medication with less negative impact on desire. The physician recommended Connor slowly wean himself off medication and monitor any changes in mood. Anti-depressant medication can be a valuable resource, especially when dealing with acute depressive feelings and stress, but Connor's use of the medication had the unintended side-effect of reinforcing his self-image as a depressed man. Connor uses all his psychosocial resources to promote positive self-esteem and personal, relational, and family goals.

Socially/relationally, Connor and Miranda worked as a team to promote personal and relational well-being. This was particularly meaningful to Connor, who saw Miranda as the most supportive person in his life. When he experienced problems, he trusted that Miranda "had his back". Connor did not want to make unrealistic promises or have a "magical" self-esteem. What Miranda provided was what Connor needed; respect and love with acceptance of Connor's strengths and vulnerabilities. This marriage brought out the best in Connor.

The marriage provided Miranda with a realistic foundation for family, home, and financial security. Even more important, Miranda felt a genuine loving bond. This marriage met her needs for intimacy and security.

Miranda was positive about sexuality. In her first marriage and subsequent dating relationships, sex started in a romantic, frequent manner but quickly degenerated into a disappointing intercourse routine. Miranda had orgasms, but felt low desire and satisfaction. She'd lost her sexual voice.

Connor loved and valued Miranda. Sexuality was a process of sharing pleasure and eroticism. Connor enjoyed sharing sexuality, not pressuring Miranda to perform so he would feel like a real man. Sex is not the most important thing in their marriage nor does Miranda view sex as compensation for the past. Sexuality is about energizing their bond and allowing each to feel desire and desirability.

Feeling like a first-class sexual man and couple is particularly important for Connor. A previous vulnerability was feeling not good enough. The theme of not being good sexually was hammered home by his ex-wife. In this marriage, both Connor and Miranda embraced Good Enough Sex (GES). Miranda felt valued and Connor felt sexually welcomed.

Miranda and Connor had a satisfying (not perfect), secure (based on acceptance), and sexual (based on GES) marriage.

## Exercise: Embracing the Psychobiosocial Model for Understanding and Change

This couple exercise focuses on changing at least one factor from each dimension. Be honest with yourself and your partner. Psychologically, what are your strengths and vulnerabilities as an individual and couple? Bio-medically, what are your strengths and vulnerabilities individually and as a couple? Socially/relationally what are your strengths and vulnerabilities individually and as a couple? Write down at least two and up to five positive factors for each dimension. This is the foundation for acceptance.

The second part of this exercise is challenging. Each partner chooses one psychological, one bio-medical, and one social/relational factor to change over the next year. Be specific about the change goal, what resources you will need to successfully implement the change, and requests of the partner to promote the change. Remember, change is a one—two process of personal responsibility and being an intimate team who work together to promote change. Change is based on a positive influence process and realistic goals.

Examples of psychological interventions include reading a scientifically validated article on sexual desire, listening to a CD or watching a DVD about couple sexuality, talking to your minister/rabbi about a pro-sexual religious perspective, using a body lotion for pleasuring, disclosing a negative sexual experience and how the partner can help in your healing process, confronting feelings of guilt or shame, talking about your most positive couple sexual experience, discussing a sex myth and how to change your reaction to it, asking a sibling his experience of learning about sexuality from your parents, and recognizing that masturbation and sexual fantasies are normal—not deviant.

Examples of bio-medical changes are not drinking before sex (or having just one drink), going for walks as a couple three times a week, discussing all your medications with your internist and changing any that have a negative sexual impact, doing an internet search on how to sexually cope with your illness or disability, scheduling a couple consultation with the medical specialist focused on understanding how to be a good patient with reduced sexual side-effects, changing sleep patterns to enhance both physical and sexual health, adopt a positive body image as part of recovery from breast cancer, discuss with your partner resources you need to understand and resources you need to restore sexuality after prostate cancer.

Relationally, rather than the traditional focus on relationship issues first and sex second, adopt a "both—and" approach to relational and sexual issues. Examples of change goals are finding a new balance of intimacy and eroticism, each partner becoming comfortable saying "no" to intercourse and offering an alternative erotic scenario, using touching to reconnect after an argument, developing a new initiation pattern, creating one to two afterplay scenarios, enjoying a sensual or playful date with a prohibition on intercourse, using self-stimulation during couple sex, transitioning to a "trust" position if an encounter does not go well.

This exercise asks you to operationalize the psychobiosocial model to increase awareness and facilitate sexual change. By its nature couple sexuality is a complex, multi-dimensional experience with a range of roles, meanings, and outcomes. The psychobiosocial model promotes desire/pleasure/eroticism/satisfaction.

## Summary

The media treats sex in a simplistic, judgmental manner. The psychobiosocial model explores the complexity of sexuality in terms of understanding, assessment, and treatment. Rather than emphasizing bio-medical factors, the key factors are psychological, especially for the core dimension of desire. We advocate the psychobiosocial model for understanding and changing sexual attitudes, behavior, and emotions. Even when there are bio-medical or social problems, the motivation for change is grounded in psychological factors.

The psychobiosocial model empowers you to understand the complexity of sexuality (especially couple sexuality) with the range of roles, meanings, and outcomes. Own your sexuality so that it has a positive 15–20% role in your life and relationship.

# 4

# FEMALE—MALE SEXUAL EQUITY

The traditional double standard has and continues to dominate sexual discourse in the United States and throughout the world. The assumption is that men and women are very different. The "common sense" belief is that male sex, especially spontaneous erections with totally predictable intercourse and orgasm, is the "right" way to have sex (Zilbergeld, 1999).

We advocate a new model: female—male sexual equity. The equity model is based on the scientific data that in adult relationships there are more sexual similarities than differences between women and men. Both genders endorse desire/pleasure/eroticism/satisfaction. Both female and male sexuality are healthy and first class. Female sexuality is more variable, flexible, complex, and individualistic, but not inferior (Brotto, 2018).

The female—male equity model is healthy for the woman, man, couple, and culture. This facilitates being intimate and erotic allies who create strong, resilient sexual desire. Rather than being stuck in the traditional male—female power struggle over "intercourse or nothing", both partners value affection, and sensual, playful, erotic, and intercourse touch. In the equity model, women and men are treated as first class sexual people. Sex is neither a performance nor a competition. Each partner recognizes and accepts that in an adult sexual relationship there are many more similarities between the genders. Differences are acknowledged and honored. You remain intimate and erotic friends. The adolescent/young adult learnings about spontaneous erections and "working on" the woman to arouse her for intercourse are discarded. The traditional double standard is replaced by sharing intimacy, pleasuring, and eroticism.

The gender split was women valued affection and relational stability while men valued eroticism and intercourse frequency. Men were the sexual initiators, women the sexual gatekeepers. The only "real" sex was intercourse. The most important (and destructive) sexual learning was that male sexual response was autonomous and natural, and healthy female sexuality was inferior. "Pop psych" books held that men and women came from different planets.

The double standard not only had major negative impacts on women; it also caused major problems for men, couples, and the culture. The only advantage of the double-standard is that the gender roles are clear. In every other way, the double standard is destructive psychologically, relationally, and sexually. The double standard negates the complexity of women, men, and couples. It ignores the inherent flexibility and variability of couple sexuality. It puts men in a narrow, performance-oriented box. It makes the woman a "sex object" and robs her of sexual autonomy.

The opposite extreme is the 50–50 equality model. This model believes that men and women are totally the same, and everything relationally and sexually needs to be split 50–50. A silly example is three days a week the woman cooks, three days a week the man cooks, and they eat out once a week. The 50–50 equality model is better than the double standard, but has major flaws. The biggest is it negates autonomy, individual differences, and complexity. The science is clear that among adults there are many more sexual similarities than differences between women and men. Yet, there are differences to be acknowledged rather than demanding 50–50 equality. In addition, individuals have their own strengths, preferences, and vulnerabilities which need to be addressed rather than ignored.

A key concept in the equity model is that both the woman and man value desire/pleasure/eroticism/satisfaction. They are intimate and erotic friends rather than the traditional gender split. Both partners value intimacy, pleasuring, and eroticism. The equity model promotes variable, flexible couple sexuality. Each person has their sexual voice, which allows them to be a unique, sexual person rather than controlled by rigid gender expectations.

The equity model is a challenge for the woman, man, couple, and culture, but a challenge worth meeting. Successful implementation of the equity model requires thought, communication, negotiation, and practice. Rather than "natural" or simple, this requires mindfulness, dialogue, and motivation. A key is viewing your partner as your intimate and erotic ally. Many women approach their partner as their intimate ally, but feel de-eroticized in the relationship. The equity model honors eroticism for the woman, man, and couple. Eroticism is integrated into the desire/pleasure/eroticism/satisfaction mantra.

## Honoring Sexual Differences

Women and men experienced very different sexual socialization, especially in adolescence and young adulthood. Although both genders experience their first orgasm with masturbation, male masturbation is easier and more frequent (Barbach, 1975). Men experience spontaneous erections and male genitalia is easily accessible. Females are taught to be wary of sex because of feared biological (pregnancy) and social (negative labels) consequences while men are encouraged to be sexually free and experimental. Most males learn sexual response as autonomous (he experiences desire, erection, and orgasm without needing anything from his partner). The vast majority of women learn sexual response as an intimate, interactive experience (Nagoski, 2015).

As adults, developing a couple sexual style which recognizes each person's sexual autonomy ("sexual voice") and promotes being an intimate sexual team is the optimal strategy. As an equitable couple, you share intimacy, pleasuring, and eroticism. Particularly important is awareness that desire and satisfaction are the core dimensions of couple sexuality. The equity model affirms both the value of each partner's sexual voice and being an intimate sexual team. Each partner has the freedom to initiate and the power to say "no" or veto a sexual scenario. Freedom and flexibility promotes sexual desire and allows you to be your authentic sexual self rather than getting caught in the narrow roles of the double standard or the rigidity of the equality model. You are not clones of each other. Respect each partner's sexual preferences and feelings rather than being controlled by gender stereotypes. A valuable psychosexual skill exercise to promote desire is to create your preferred sexual scenario. This makes personal and concrete a core advantage of the equity model. Your preferred way of initiating, pleasuring, eroticism, intercourse, orgasm, and afterplay is almost certainly different than your partner's. Accepting and honoring differences promotes strong, resilient desire for both partners. Female—male sexual equity is not an abstract "politically correct" approach, but a cognitive, behavioral, emotional integration.

## Gloria and Blake

Gloria and Blake were in their early 30s and had been together for eight years, five as a married couple. They have fond memories of their 19-month limerance phase, but by the time of marriage they had settled into a traditional double standard approach to sex, especially initiation. Gloria enjoyed their sexual relationship, including orgasm, but thought of Blake as the more sexual partner. All of Blake's initiations resulted in intercourse, so Gloria was forced into the role of sexual gatekeeper. Their sexual routine was functional, but not vital or satisfying. Over time Gloria's sexual desire had become muted. Blake reacted by spending more time with foreplay, where he stimulated her breasts and vulva to get her ready for intercourse. Gloria settled into a passive role. Like the majority of women, Gloria could be orgasmic with both intercourse and erotic stimulation (manual and oral). Early in the relationship she reached orgasm before intercourse, which made intercourse more pleasurable. Blake values Gloria being orgasmic during intercourse, so this became their primary pattern. Gloria would fake orgasms so Blake could let go and ejaculate. Gloria viewed Blake as a spouse who cared for her, but cared about intercourse frequency and performance more. Like one in three women Gloria was now experiencing low sexual desire. She had good memories of how their sexual relationship had been, but was not enjoying it now. Increasingly, she focused on parenting, the house, and friends, and less on Blake, and certainly not on sexuality.

Gloria and Blake had fallen into the traditional male—female power struggle over intercourse frequency. When speaking with male friends,

Blake had two standard lines—"Marriage kills sex" and "Any sex is good sex". Rather than being intimate and erotic allies, they were each other's critics. Blake tried to be her caring lover, but felt Gloria had shut down sexually. Gloria felt they were a good couple and good family, but that Blake's intercourse obsession was off-putting. Every time he touched her it resulted in a struggle over intercourse.

This pattern was disrupted by a crisis. Gloria came home late from a community meeting to discover Blake asleep with the computer open to a porn site. Gloria knew that Blake occasionally masturbated and believed that was normal for men (she had masturbated as a young adult woman but not now). However, she was appalled by seeing semen on his thigh and porn on the computer. She woke Blake and told him to take a shower. Gloria would not speak to him when he came to bed. The next morning Blake was embarrassed and apologetic, but when Gloria still wouldn't speak he became angry. They traded accusations and put-downs, which both later regretted.

It was Gloria who suggested consulting a couple therapist with a specialty in sex therapy. The therapist asked that both attend the first session because intimacy and sexuality are best approached as a couple issue. Gloria was reluctant, feeling that sex was Blake's problem—both porn and intercourse pressure. Blake was on the defensive, ready to defend himself against a charge of "sex addiction". They were surprised by the therapist's question "When did sexuality have a positive role in your relationship?" Both recalled the limerance phase where touching and sexuality were special and powerful. The therapist acknowledged this and that it must be sad that now sex was a battleground and disappointment. In many ways, they were friends and partners, but sexuality was a source of conflict and alienation.

There is something about sex problems which brings out the worst in people, especially defensiveness and the urge to counterattack. This point hit home with Blake. He was genuinely embarrassed and regretful about being discovered after masturbating to porn. He felt humiliated and shamed by Gloria. This caused him to counterattack, which made the situation worse. Attacking Gloria as "frigid" and blaming her for his masturbation and porn use was unfair and destructive. Blake did not feel shamed by the therapist. He realized telling Gloria "just do it" was not the answer to their sexual problems.

The therapist asked Gloria when she stopped thinking of Blake as her sexual friend. She admitted that after the limerance phase, she no longer thought of him as her erotic ally. Gloria viewed Blake as a sex-obsessed husband who cared about intercourse frequency, not her feelings or desire for intimacy. Blake was surprised and hurt, but assured Gloria it wasn't true. He emphasized the time and effort he devoted to foreplay, so she could have an orgasm during intercourse. Gloria began to counter-attack about sex technique, but the clinician asked that she be aware of Blake's positive intentions.

The therapist observed that Gloria and Blake were trapped in the power struggle of who was the "bad spouse". No one wins a power struggle, it is about who is the "loser". The power struggle cycle has a life of its own and was destructive for Blake, Gloria, and their marriage.

The clinician's role is not to judge or referee; it is to promote an empathic, respectful, intimate relationship. In addition, it is to help Gloria and Blake create an equitable couple sexual style so that they again feel like allies. The couple challenge is to build strong, resilient sexual desire so that sexuality has a positive 15–20% role in their relationship. Gloria found this description of therapy motivating, but feared they would not be able to meet it. Blake said it made a lot of sense, but Gloria had to stop demonizing him. The therapist warned Blake against "tit for tat" arguments. He needed to be responsible for his behavior (emotionally and sexually), including not counter-attacking. There is nothing to gain in a power struggle.

Rather than the traditional approach of focusing on individual issues first, then relationship issues, and finally sexual issues, the couple therapist adopted the "both—and" approach of focusing on personal, relational, and sexual issues in an integrated manner. The equity model was explored with its role in their emotional and sexual relationship. Gloria and Blake decided on the Best Friend relational style. This is the most common couple choice because it affirms the role of marriage to meet needs for intimacy and security. Blake trusted "Gloria has my back". Gloria felt that Blake again respected her as a person.

The issue of their couple sexual style was more challenging. Gloria assumed it would be the same as their relational style, a Best Friend sexual style based on a close, intimate connection. The therapist challenged Gloria and Blake to find the right sexual style for them, and made them aware that often the couple sexual style is different than the relational style. Sexual style refers to how each partner maintains their "sexual voice" (autonomy) while being a sexual team who integrate intimacy and eroticism. Gloria found Blake's focus on intercourse frequency and his need for her to be orgasmic during intercourse unwanted pressure and a turn-off. Gloria did not see him as her sexual ally. Blake said he wanted to be her sexual friend, but was at a loss of what he could do. His fear was that she wanted him to accept a non-sexual marriage. Gloria was surprised to hear that because it was the opposite of her goal. However, Gloria admitted that she had lost her sexual voice and was unsure of how to be an equitable sexual couple.

The therapist suggested they focus on the desire psychosexual skill exercises of comfort, attraction, trust, and create your own scenario (McCarthy & McCarthy, 2012). They began with the attraction exercise, which involved two phases. Gloria began by stating the emotional, physical, social, sexual, and parental characteristics that she found attractive about Blake. It was important that Gloria be genuine, not give socially desirable answers. Blake needed to accept what she said, not minimize it. Then Gloria made requests which would increase Blake's attractiveness to her. These are requests, not demands. Gloria had two requests—engage in non-sexual touching and allow multiple stimulation during intercourse. She was surprised when he endorsed both her requests. Blake wanted to be her sexual friend rather than judge her sexual response.

Then Blake made a list of what he found attractive about Gloria. She was surprised by the range of factors he valued, especially relational and emotional dimensions. This confronted her resentment that all he cared about was intercourse. Blake's two requests were to love him and stop calling him a "porn addict".

The comfort exercise involved giving and receiving touching where the focus was on pleasure and connection rather than intercourse.

Blake and Gloria had fallen into the traditional gender trap of splitting intimacy (Gloria) and eroticism (Blake). In addition, sex was defined as intercourse, so they stayed stuck in the "intercourse or nothing" struggle.

Therapy and the psychosexual skill exercises encouraged Gloria and Blake to create a dialogue about the role of intimacy, pleasuring, and eroticism in their marriage. The biggest challenge for Gloria was to find her "erotic voice" and give up her resentment over his porn use and intercourse pressure. Blake's agreement to set boundaries about masturbation and use of erotic materials was reassuring to Gloria. The challenge for Blake was to acknowledge that sensual, playful, and erotic scenarios were healthy ways to express sexuality. Sex involves intercourse, but sexuality is more than intercourse. Blake needed to be aware that female sexuality was healthy—more variable, flexible, complex, and individualistic, but not inferior.

Especially important was adopting the Good Enough Sex (GES) model of sharing pleasure as a couple. This meant giving up the demand that each sexual encounter involve intercourse, with Gloria being orgasmic during intercourse. Blake learned that a "wise" man accepts his partner and her unique desire/pleasure/eroticism/satisfaction pattern. Gloria's desire was "responsive" rather than Blake's pattern of spontaneous desire signaled by an erection. Her pleasuring pattern includes giving and receiving stimulation, not being passive during foreplay.

In retrospect, the "foreplay" scenario was a turn-off for Gloria. This was new, crucial information for Blake. Gloria was not responsive to breast or vulva stimulation until her subjective arousal was at least a "5" and preferably a "6" (on a 10-point scale of arousal). Although Gloria could be orgasmic during intercourse and valued a "vaginal" orgasm, she found it easier and preferable to be orgasmic with manual or oral stimulation before intercourse. This was new information for Blake.

Gloria had specific requests about afterplay. Her first request was negative: "Don't ask me whether I came". Her positive request was to create at least one new afterplay scenario. Blake thought of afterplay as being for Gloria—holding, a kiss, "I love you", and sleep. Gloria wanted more for herself and them as a couple. She wanted to feel a genuine connection which affirmed her as a sexual woman and them as an intimate sexual couple. It took Gloria and Blake three weeks to create an afterplay scenario which felt genuine and affirming. This was a very valuable resource for their marriage and couple sexuality.

In retrospect, even at the beginning of their relationship, Blake and Gloria never felt like an equitable couple. Sex was Blake's domain rather than sexuality as a shared pleasure.

Blake and Gloria not only survived the relationship crisis; they were genuine intimate and erotic allies. They were a respectful, trusting, intimate, and equitable team. Gloria had feared she would have to give up her autonomy, but now realized her strong self-esteem was good for their marriage. This was reinforced by Blake's respect for her. Equity does not mean giving up your sexual self. It involves respecting yourself with your psychological, relational, and sexual strengths and vulnerabilities. Your partner accepts, respects, and loves you for who you really are (your authentic self). This allows you to accept yourself as a sexual woman and feel accepted by your partner as his intimate and erotic ally.

Blake's fear about the equity model was that he would have to sacrifice his sexuality or settle for a feminized sense of sex. Instead, Blake felt more accepting of himself as a sexual man and them as a sexual couple. Rather than a secret life of masturbation and porn, he valued Gloria and couple sexuality. Blake accepted the multiple roles, meanings, and outcomes of sexuality. Both Blake and Gloria valued integrated eroticism and accepted masturbation and erotic fantasies as long as it wasn't at the expense of the partner or their relationship. Porn is harmful when it involves secrecy, a narrow view of eroticism, and shame—this combination is a "poison". Blake and Gloria accepted that porn is an erotic fantasy dimension which has nothing to do with real life couple sexuality. Gloria accepting that porn was not a negation of her or couple sexuality allowed Blake to feel positive about eroticism in his life and relationship.

An equitable female—male sexual relationship does not mean you are clones of one another. Equity means you recognize similarities and differences, and affirm that you deserve sexuality to have a 15–20% positive role in your relationship.

Gloria and Blake wish it hadn't taken a crisis for them to challenge their sexual behaviors and values, but were proud they had met the challenge. They created an equitable sexual relationship which enhanced desire/pleasure/eroticism/satisfaction.

## Barriers to an Equitable Sexual Relationship

The biggest barrier to an equitable sexual relationship is inertia. People continue overlearned habits. Traditional gender roles are powerfully overlearned in the family, especially adolescent and young adult socialization. It is easy to go with the "tried and true". Easy, but very unwise. Traditional gender roles inhibit the growth of women, men, couples, and the culture.

The equity model is a challenge; a challenge worth meeting. The personal barrier is the fear of losing something. The relational barrier is the amount of time, energy, and communication necessary to successfully implement the equity model. The cultural barrier is over reliance on conservative family and religious traditions. Traditionalists fear disruptions to the family and the culture.

Change does entail risks. Fears of poor choices and confusion are realistic. However, in the case of gender equity there is a positive model of change which has scientific validation. The science is clear that adults, especially those who are well-educated and in a relationship, share many more similarities intellectually, behaviorally, emotionally, and sexually than differences. Differences are accepted and honored, but be aware there are more individual than gender differences.

Be honest with yourself and share psychological, relational, and sexual strengths and vulnerabilities. Rather than gender stereotypes, be personal and concrete about who you are in terms of attitudes, feelings, behaviors, preferences, and values. This asks a lot of both partners, but goes a long way toward establishing and maintaining a genuine, equitable relationship.

## Exercise: Creating a Genuine Equitable Relationship

The first step in this exercise is to make a conscious decision of whether you value and want a genuine equitable relationship. Do both partners affirm this as a personally relevant goal?

Next, discuss relational models, especially your parents. Do you have a positive model for an equitable relationship or will you need to put time, energy, and thought into creating your own model?

What do you respect about yourself as a person? Have you shared this with your partner? What is your major vulnerability? Is that vulnerability changeable, modifiable, or do you and your partner need to accept and work around it? In an equitable relationship you feel accepted, respected, and loved for who you really are with your vulnerabilities as well as strengths.

Next, focus on your relational history. How did you begin as a couple? Did you start as a double standard couple, a 50–50 couple, an unfocused relational pattern, or an equitable couple? Interestingly, few couples begin in an equitable mode. Many fall into a double standard where tasks and domains are divided along traditional gender roles. Other couples give gender roles little thought and do whatever comes, usually in a disorganized manner.

Your power to change is in the present and future. You can learn from the past, but cannot change it. It does you no good to engage in "what if" or "should have" thinking. Even less helpful is to reinforce feelings of hurt, resentment, or anger about past relational and sexual inequity.

Are you motivated and committed to creating an equitable relationship in the present? Will you devote the time and energy to dialogue about what it means to be an equitable couple? For some, the key is to increase respect for your partner and relationship. For others, it is to build a genuine trust bond. For still others, it is to establish a new couple sexual style where both partners value intimacy and eroticism. Many couples focus on all those issues in developing an equitable relationship. The core of a healthy marriage (life partnership) is creating a respectful, trusting, intimate commitment. This means accepting that all people and all relationships have strengths and vulnerabilities. A core factor in an equitable relationship is acceptance of self and partner. This contrasts with a contingent sexual self-esteem or a contingent relationship. To make this real and concrete, share with your partner psychological, relational, or sexual information you have kept secret. This means sharing the themes and meanings of experiences, but not getting stuck in the details. Themes free the person and relationship, details keep you stuck in the past and reinforce stigma and blame. Typically, the partner is more accepting of the sensitive or secret material than the person. Self-acceptance and partner acceptance facilitate sexual self-esteem and a genuine equitable relationship.

Acknowledging personal, partner, and relational strengths enhances your equitable relationship. Healthy emotional and sexual relationships live the five to one guideline. This means five positive attitudes, behaviors, and feelings mixed with one negative. This five to one ratio facilitates feeling respected and loved while addressing issues and vulnerabilities. Equitable relationships are anti-perfectionism. They are positive and realistic, not magical. They do not utilize the "If you loved me you would" approach. Equitable relationships recognize that you are not clones of each other. Differences are honored—they add spice and vitality to your lives.

To make this personal and concrete, each partner lists and shares positive thoughts, feelings, and experiences you value about each other. Then discuss concerns and difficulties, ensuring you stay within the five to one ratio. With the negatives, are these changeable, modifiable, or do they need to be accepted and worked around? Be aware that even in the most loving relationship, there will be at least one vulnerability or negative which is not changeable.

The last task in this exercise is to create a maintenance/relapse prevention plan so that you continue an equitable, satisfying (not perfect) relationship. A common strategy is to have a dialogue every six months about the state of your intimate relationship to ensure it remains vital and satisfying. In addition, set a new growth goal for the next six months. The growth goal can be individual or relational. You cannot treat your relationship or sex in your relationship with benign neglect. Examples of growth goals include developing a new afterplay scenario, planning a child-free couple weekend, becoming comfortable with a new intercourse position or a multiple stimulation scenario during intercourse, revisiting your favorite small town or museum, asking your spouse to support you when you have a difficult conversation with a sibling, or together purchasing a sexually seductive outfit or a new body lotion. Your intimate sexual relationship needs new inputs and energy.

## Summary

Creating and maintaining an equitable relationship is a worthwhile challenge for the woman, man, and couple. It is not enough to reject the double standard; you need to establish a genuine sense of equity. This is much more challenging than just saying the words and having good intentions. This is especially true since our culture does not promote equity between women and men. There are relatively few good models, especially of sexual equity. Traditional gender stereotypes are overlearned and die hard. It's easy to rebel against the double standard; the challenge is to create and maintain genuine equity.

Intellectually, physically, emotionally, behaviorally, relationally, and sexually there are many more similarities than differences between adult women and men. An equitable relationship is good for the woman, man, couple, and culture. You owe it to yourself, your partner, and your children to embrace female—male equity.

# 5

# DIMENSIONS OF TOUCH, PLEASURE, AND SEXUALITY

Sadly, the great majority of couples only utilize two dimensions of touch—affection and intercourse. This results in the "intercourse or nothing" approach to sex. The male—female power struggle is whether you will have sex—defined as intercourse. When it's "intercourse or nothing", nothing usually wins.

Couples who have been together for two years or longer have intercourse on average 59–62 times a year, a bit more than once a week. The average range of intercourse frequency is between 3–12 times a month. A low sex relationship involves intercourse between 11–23 times a year. A non-sexual relationship is defined as having intercourse less than ten times a year. Approximately one in five married couples and an even larger number of partnered and cohabitating couples have a non-sexual relationship. Contrary to media myths, Americans are not having an abundance of sex (Laumann et al., 1994).

We explore a motivating, empowering new model of touch, pleasure, and sexuality. There are five dimensions of touch—affection, sensual, playful, erotic, and intercourse (McCarthy & McCarthy, 2012). An analogy is the five gears (dimensions) of a stick shift car—each touch gear has a valuable role.

The core of couple sexuality is giving and receiving pleasure-oriented touch. In understanding the five dimensions (gears) of touch a helpful concept is levels of pleasure (subjective arousal). The scale is 0 (neutral) to 10 (orgasm). Affectionate touch anchors the couple at 1. Affectionate touch is not sexual, rather holding hands, kissing, and hugging create feelings of attachment. The other four dimensions—sensual, playful, erotic, and intercourse—are all forms of sexual expression. Sexuality is much more than intercourse.

Sensual touch involves giving and receiving pleasure; subjective pleasure/arousal is in the 1–3 range. Examples include non-genital body massage, cuddling on the couch listening to a CD or watching a DVD, touching when going to sleep or on awakening. Sensual touch can be mutual, taking turns, or one-way. Sensual touching allows you to be sexual in a sensual manner.

Playful touch mixes genital and non-genital touching; subjective pleasure/arousal is in the 4–5 range. Examples include whole body massage (including genitals), touching while bathing or showering, dancing in a romantic or seductive manner, playing a game like strip poker or Twister, or "making out". Playful touch is usually mutual. It can be clothed, semi-clothed, or nude. You are being sexual in a playful manner.

Sensual and playful touch are in the category of the non-demand pleasuring dimension. Pleasuring is valuable for both partners, whether for itself or as a bridge to arousal and intercourse.

The fourth dimension, erotic touch, is the most challenging and potentially contentious. In terms of pleasure/subjective arousal this involves 6–10 sensations/feelings. The most common type of erotic touch is manual stimulation, next oral stimulation, followed by rubbing stimulation, and then vibrator stimulation. The erotic scenario can be mutual and synchronous or asynchronous (better for one partner than the other). Although couples prefer synchronous sexual experiences, asynchronous sexuality is normal and healthy as long as it's not at the expense of the partner or relationship.

Erotic touch is healthy sexuality for the woman, man, and couple. It can involve orgasm for one or both partners, but not as a performance goal. The core of erotic sexuality is experiencing intensely pleasurable feelings and sensations.

What makes erotic sexuality contentious is when the focus is on sexual demand/performance or manipulation rather than on sharing pleasure and eroticism. The foundation for healthy couple sexuality is pleasure and consent. Performance demands and coercion poison sexuality, especially desire.

Sensual, playful, and erotic touch are healthy sexual experiences for the woman, man, and couple.

The fifth dimension (gear) is intercourse. The best way to understand intercourse is as a natural continuation of the pleasuring/eroticism process. The self-defeating approach is to view intercourse as an individual pass—fail performance test. Intercourse is part of your couple repertoire, including two core guidelines. First, transition to intercourse when it makes sense sexually (subjective arousal 7–8) rather than as soon as you can. A major mistake couples make is to transition to intercourse as soon as possible (subjective arousal 4–5). The man does this because he fears losing his erection. Negative motivation does not promote healthy sexuality. The second guideline is to enjoy multiple stimulation during intercourse rather than depending solely on intercourse thrusting. Multiple stimulation involves giving and receiving pleasurable and erotic touch. The most common forms of receiving stimulation for women is clitoral stimulation, whether with his fingers, her fingers, or a vibrator; buttock or anal stimulation; and breast stimulation. For males, it is receiving testicle stimulation, buttock stimulation, and kissing stimulation. For both women and men, the most common form of multiple stimulation is private erotic fantasies which serve as a bridge to erotic flow and orgasm (Mark et al., 2014).

Intercourse is an integral component of the desire/pleasure/eroticism/satisfaction mantra; not a pass—fail individual performance test.

## Implementing the Five Dimensions of Touch, Pleasure, and Sexuality

This is not simply a change in cognitive understanding. Our approach to sexuality involves cognitive, behavioral, emotional enactment. Value affectionate, sensual, playful, erotic, and intercourse touch. It is crucial to have at least one dimension to add to affection and intercourse. More commonly one partner values four to five dimensions and the other three to four dimensions. Each partner has the right to veto a dimension, with confidence that your partner will honor that veto. This is crucial for genuine sexual openness and receptivity. Do not give the "socially desirable" response, especially when you are not comfortable implementing it. Expand your sensual and sexual repertoire. Reinforce being intimate and erotic friends who value touch, pleasure, and sexuality.

In implementing this model each partner notes the percent of affectionate, sensual, playful, erotic, and intercourse touch experienced at present. Then, your preference for types of touch. A common pattern is a request to increase affectionate, sensual, playful, and erotic touch. This is not at the expense of intercourse, but to expand your sexual repertoire. The concept of dimensions of touch facilitates freedom to connect and reconnect via touch.

Ideally, you practice each touch dimension three times to see if it is comfortable and pleasurable. Experiment to discover whether you prefer mutual touch (partner interaction arousal) or taking turns (self-entrancement arousal); clothes on or nude; talking or letting your fingers do the talking; in the bedroom or another space; music in the background or a scented candle; a planned, semi-planned, or spontaneous touching date. Many couples prefer a temporary prohibition on intercourse and/or orgasm while others go with the flow. Commonly, couples have different touching preferences. This is normal and healthy. You are not clones of each other. Each partner establishes his/her affectionate, sensual, playful, erotic, and intercourse "voice".

What do you value about touch, pleasure, and sexuality? The role of sexuality is to energize your bond and reinforce feelings of desire and desirability. Embracing the multiple roles, meanings, and outcomes of sexual touch enhances desire/pleasure/eroticism/satisfaction. Integrate the dimensions of touch in your unique manner. This includes the power to veto one and up to three touching scenarios. Whether this strategy is used or not, having this resource available is empowering. Unless you have the power to say "no" to sex you do not have the freedom to embrace intimacy, pleasure, and eroticism.

You have the right to your touch preferences and sexual voice. Each partner has both positive and negative feelings regarding touch. It's not a matter of "right" or "wrong", but acceptance of sexual differences, feelings, and values. The key to implementation is openness to experiment and discover what dimensions of touch and sexuality you are receptive and responsive to. This is crucial in individualizing your couple sexual style. Adopting the variable, flexible approach to touch, pleasure, and sexuality enhances your relationship. Recognize the multiple roles, meanings, and outcomes of sexuality rather than assuming that all sex should be mutual and have the same meaning and outcome for both partners (Metz & McCarthy, 2010).

## Synchronous and Asynchronous Sexuality

The best couple sex is mutual and synchronous. This means both partners experience desire/pleasure/eroticism/satisfaction. However, the reality is that most sexual encounters are asynchronous. This means the sexual experience is better for one partner than the other. This is not only normal, it is healthy. Rather than pretending, it allows you to enjoy your genuine sexual experience. A particularly valuable learning is to highlight an encounter where the man has an orgasm while the woman is not orgasmic, but she feels more satisfied than him. Satisfaction is more than objective sex function. Sexuality involves subjective feelings, attitudes, and preferences. As long as the asynchronous sexual experience is not at the expense of the partner or relationship it is welcomed. For example, the man finds a sensual experience (second gear) extremely satisfying, while she finds it okay but not special. Another example is the woman finds that an erotic encounter results in a multi-orgasmic response which is highly satisfying, while the man describes his orgasm as an "insignificant spasm". We purposely used non-traditional gender examples to confront "common sense" assumptions about gender and sex.

Asynchronous sexuality illustrates the difference between objective sexual response and subjective pleasure/arousal. An important learning is that subjective sexual pleasure/arousal (feeling good and responsive) is more important than objective response (erection, lubrication, and orgasm). Recognizing differences in feelings, meanings, and satisfaction affirms the multiple roles of touching and sexuality. This is such a different couple dialogue than "Are we going to have sex or not?" Sexuality is not dichotomous. It is "both—and" not "either—or". Both synchronous and asynchronous scenarios have value for the woman, man, and couple. Sensual, playful, erotic, and intercourse scenarios are valuable whether synchronous or asynchronous.

## Lydia and Marshall

Unfortunately, couples often enter sex therapy when the problem is chronic and severe rather than acute and mild. This was true of Lydia and Marshall, who had been married nine years, with chronic sexual conflict for eight years. Like most couples, Lydia and Marshall began as a romantic love/passionate sex/idealized couple. They have wonderful memories of this limerance phase. Frequency of touching and intercourse was high and touching easily transitioned to intercourse, which was mutual and synchronous. Lydia felt that sex demonstrated their love and specialness. Marshall felt he was a lucky man to have such a pro-sexual spouse. When friends complained they had to beg for sex, he felt good about the vitality and specialness of his relationship.

When the sexual "magic" disappeared, they fell into a blame—counter-blame pattern that accelerated and controlled not just their sexual relationship, but their entire relationship. When they had sex with the goal of pregnancy, good feelings were reignited. They were thrilled to have a 4-year-old daughter and an 18-month-old son. Being a four-person family reinforced their desire to be married, but the sex conflict subverted their lives. Lydia and Marshall were no longer intimate and erotic friends. Instead, they were each other's worst critic.

Lydia accused Marshall of being a sex obsessed bully. The attack which particularly hurt him was "Sex feels like you masturbate into my vagina". Her accusations felt unfair and vicious. He couldn't believe that someone who he loved and was the mother of his children could be so angry. Marshall was unsure if the sex problem was his fault. Rather than admitting his confusion, he engaged in dramatic attacks on Lydia. He accused her of pulling a sexual "bait and switch". Worse, he said this had been a planned sexual manipulation to get what she really wanted—children, not him. Lydia felt Marshall was purposefully destroying her loving feelings and good sexual memories. Sex problems bring out the worst in people. Once in the self-defeating power struggle, the cycle takes on a life of its own which becomes chronic and severe.

When Lydia and Marshall appeared at the therapist's office they were a very demoralized couple who felt there was no resolution to their sex problem. The question was, should they stay married for the sake of the children?

A prime role of the therapist is to help the couple develop positive, realistic change expectations. The clinician is empathic and respectful of both clients and their relationship while confronting the destructive blame—counter-blame cycle. This problem-solving approach was appealing to Marshall. He was afraid Lydia would leave him. Underneath his anger there was a genuine desire to stay married because he loved Lydia. Lydia was afraid that the therapist was going to negate her feelings and say "just do it". Lydia had lost her "sexual voice" so intercourse was unappealing, and she felt trapped in the "intercourse or nothing" power struggle.

In the first couple session, the therapist was clear that he would attend to all five clients: (1) Lydia, (2) Marshall, (3) their relationship, (4) their sexual relationship, and (5) the hardest client—their emotional and sexual history as a couple. The therapist emphasized that although they could learn from the past, their power to change is in the present and future. Refighting the details of the past eight years would only keep them stuck. In many areas of their relationship they positively influenced each other, but sexually they were critical and destructive.

The next step in the assessment process was the individual psychological/relational/sexual history. If the history is conducted with the spouse present it will result in a "sanitized" version rather than the genuine narrative. The majority of clients have past or present sensitive/secret material that has not been shared with the partner (McCarthy, 2002). For Marshall, sensitive issues were his masturbation frequency and going to strip bars. Sensitive issues for Lydia were that she had contacted a divorce attorney and fantasized about acting out a "crush" with a neighbor. Both Marshall and Lydia felt shame about their thoughts and actions, and feared the other's judgment. In many areas they had a good life, but the state of intimacy and sexuality was quite sad.

In the couple feedback session, the therapist recommended they commit to a six-month "good faith" effort to rebuild their bond and develop a new couple sexual style. He emphasized that they needed to learn from the past, but they couldn't have a makeover. The power of change is in the present and future.

The fact that they experienced a limerance phase was a good prognostic sign, but they could not return to romantic love/passionate sex. It is a joint challenge to develop a new couple sexual style which values desire/pleasure/eroticism/satisfaction. The therapist reassured Lydia that the sexual focus would be on touching and pleasuring which included intercourse, but intercourse was not the sole focus or even the most important factor. Giving and receiving pleasure-oriented touch would be the focus of their new couple sexual style. The therapist turned to Marshall and asked whether that made sense. Marshall shocked Lydia by affirming that focus.

Marshall was surprised and pleased that the therapist was empathic and respectful rather than demonizing him. Men are often treated as second class citizens in therapy, blamed for not disclosing feelings. Often, the therapist sides with the woman and calls the man a "Neanderthal". Feeling respected allowed Marshall to reengage with his wife, rather than feeling he was going to be emotionally beaten up in therapy.

The therapist was clear about how destructive the power struggle was; it "poisoned" their relationship. Power struggles are not about winning or moving forward, they are about who is the "bad spouse". Marshall affirmed this approach and committed to stop blaming sexual problems on Lydia. Even if she accused him of something, he would not retaliate. Lydia was hesitant, but reassured that her feelings would be heard and honored in therapy and in the marriage.

At the end of the feedback session, the therapist described the first psychosexual skill exercise to be done in the privacy of their home. There is no touching, nudity, or sexuality in the therapist's office. Half the therapy occurs at their home where touching, nudity, and sexuality is featured in the psychosexual skill exercises. The first exercise was to develop a trust position where they felt secure and attached. Ideally, this is done in the privacy of their bedroom (door locked) or when children are out of the house. The focus is to reestablish touch without the pressure of "intercourse or nothing". The trust position Lydia and Marshall developed was her lying on his shoulder with his arm around her back. They decided not to talk in the trust position, but to be with each other in a sensual, warm manner. There was no expectation of arousal; the focus was on attachment and safety. The trust exercise is an anti-avoidance strategy to get Lydia and Marshall re-involved in pleasure-oriented touching.

The second psychosexual skill exercise involved building comfort with sensual touch. Lydia and Marshall experimented with mutual touch vs. taking turns; talking while touching or letting their fingers do the talking; touching while clothed vs. nude; using a sensual lotion or natural touching; having music in the background to facilitate the milieu; touching in the family room vs. the bedroom. The focus is non-genital pleasuring with pleasure/subjective arousal in the 1–3 range. Lydia was particularly pleased with this exercise—she enjoyed Marshall's touch without fear of sexual pressure. Mutual touch was most inviting. Like most males, Marshall had not valued sensual touch, seeing it as a feminine experience. Marshall learned to value sensual touch for himself, especially being in the receiving role. He no longer viewed sensuality as feminine or a way to avoid intercourse. Marshall had built sexual resentment and did not trust Lydia's motivation. The non-demand pleasuring exercises were emotionally healing for Marshall, allowing him to feel genuinely attached and building confidence that they were an intimate sexual team. The biggest difference for Lydia was realizing that Marshall's erection was not a pressure to perform. Lydia realized that their traditional foreplay scenario, where she was passive while Marshall tried to arouse her, was a turn-off that made her resent sex. Lydia appreciated that Marshall was open and experimental.

Lydia respected Marshall, but had not seen him as her sexual ally. She thought of him as sexually needy and selfish. Now she understood erection as a natural response to pleasure. Touching was a shared pleasure, not a sexual demand. This was reinforced when Marshall promised that he would not sexually coerce her.

Both in therapy sessions and at home, Lydia and Marshall affirmed that sensual, playful, erotic, and intercourse touch were healthy ways to express sexuality. Marshall was least enthusiastic about playful touch, but since Lydia found it so fulfilling he learned to enjoy this touch dimension.

At first Lydia did not value asynchronous erotic sex, especially when Marshall was the receiving partner. After three to four experiences, she understood that she wasn't "servicing" him, but that he enjoyed her pleasuring him to orgasm. What made this clear was the experience and sensations Lydia felt when Marshall pleasured her to orgasm. Asynchronous sexual experiences are normal and healthy and became an integral part of their sexual repertoire. Feeling demanded on or coerced is not acceptable. Pleasuring the partner, whether with sensual, playful, erotic, or intercourse, is healthy and affirming.

The core issue was establishing that Lydia and Marshall were intimate and erotic allies. This was reinforced during therapy sessions. Engaging in sensual, playful, erotic, and intercourse psychosexual skill exercises was crucial. Breaking the sexual power struggle is necessary, but not sufficient. Embrace flexible, variable couple sexuality which includes affectionate, sensual, playful, erotic, and intercourse touch. Most important was breaking the "intercourse or nothing" pattern and recognizing that sensual, playful and erotic touch are sexual. Lydia and Marshall embraced the five dimensions of touch.

## Implementing Dimensions of Touch

Sexual learning is not just a matter of communication and changing attitudes. The change process involves cognitive, behavioral, and emotional enactment. Changing attitudes and talking about touch is necessary, but even more important is implementing these concepts into your life and relationship. An effective way to implement this is to engage in psychosexual skill exercises.

## Five Psychosexual Skill Exercises

We suggest scheduling two to three dates for each dimension of touch. We recommend doing each gear in order, although if you like being adventurous you can mix up the order. The reason we suggest at least two and preferably three practices is to give you the opportunity to develop comfort and confidence with each dimension. Many people report awkwardness/discomfort the first time, but with practice find that each touch gear (dimension) is valuable.

We present guidelines rather than a rigid cookbook. The focus is sharing pleasure and building confidence. Remember, the partner has the right to veto anything which is uncomfortable, but no more than three vetoes. Give yourself and your relationship freedom to enjoy touch and share pleasure.

### Gear 1—Affectionate Touch

Do this with clothes on—hold hands, kiss, hug—enjoy affectionate touch. This promotes attachment and pleasure. Affectionate touch is not sexual, but it anchors you at 1, establishing a genuine connection. Experiment with mutual vs. one-way touch, talking vs. being silent, silly vs. intimate touch. Some couples discover one partner is a kisser and the other a hugger—this is normal and healthy. You are not clones.

### Gear 2—Sensual Touch

This is the beginning sexual dimension focused on non-genital touch with subjective pleasure/arousal in the 1–3 range. Experiment with one-way vs. mutual, verbal vs. non-verbal, a lotion or not, candles or dimmed lighting to create a sensual mood. Try long, slow, rhythmic stroking over your partner's whole body (except for breasts and genitals). Don't second guess your partner—touch for yourself. In subsequent exercises your partner will guide you. Enjoy the touching experience, not to turn your partner on, but to enjoy giving and receiving pleasure-oriented touch. You are sharing sexuality in a sensual manner.

### Gear 3—Playful Touch

Focus on mixing non-genital and genital touch with subjective pleasure/arousal of 4–5. Playful touch is part of nondemand pleasuring. Playful touch can include whole body massage, touching while showering or bathing, dancing in a romantic or seductive manner, playing a silly game like strip poker or Twister. A key to playful touch is accepting sexual responsivity (erection and vaginal lubrication) without feeling pressured. This is especially valuable for the woman. So many women are turned off by the man's erection rather than welcoming it as a symbol of pleasure.

Embrace playful touch as integral to sexuality. This is the touch dimension most likely to be skipped because it feels awkward, neither sensual nor erotic. Be open and experiment to see if playful touch can be a valued addition to your couple repertoire. Playfulness is a special relational dimension. For playfulness to exist there needs to be genuine trust and attachment, which allows you to take risks and feel accepting whether it's a great or dud experience. Playfulness requires self-acceptance and partner acceptance.

### Gear 4—Erotic Touch

Erotic touch—manual, oral, rubbing, or vibrator stimulation—is the most contentious and potentially problematic touch dimension. Traditionally, erotic touch had been to service the partner if intercourse fails or one partner does not want intercourse.

In our dimensions of touch model, erotic touch is experienced differently. Integrated eroticism is valuable for the woman, man, and couple. Subjective pleasure/arousal is in the 6–10 range. Although erotic touch usually transitions to intercourse, erotic touch is valuable whether or not it involves intercourse or orgasm. Most people enjoy receiving manual stimulation, others prefer oral stimulation, and still others prefer being active in rubbing stimulation. Erotic stimulation is usually mutual, but some couples value self-entrancement arousal, especially one partner pleasuring the other to orgasm. This is totally different than "servicing" the partner or feeling pressured to provide an orgasm. This sexual scenario is asynchronous, but good for both the giving and receiving partner. Eroticism has a bad reputation as following the porn model, male domination, or being sexually selfish. Erotic sexuality involves intense pleasure. You have a right to your "erotic voice" as long as it's not at the expense of your partner or relationship.

### Gear 5—Intercourse Touch

Intercourse is a natural extension of the pleasuring/eroticism process. Intercourse is an integral component of your relationship, not an individual pass—fail test. Intercourse is valued as a special couple experience, and you affirm sexuality is more than intercourse. This approach to intercourse allows you to be sexual in your 50s, 60s, 70s, and 80s.

In implementing this approach, we urge you to experiment with two strategies. First, transition to intercourse when it makes sexual sense, when your subjective pleasure/arousal is 7–8 rather than when you can (subjective arousal 4–5). The major reason women do not value intercourse and that men fail at Viagra is they transition at low levels of arousal. You are receptive and responsive with intercourse when she feels subjectively and objectively aroused. The man rushes to intercourse because he is afraid of losing his erection, which becomes a self-fulfilling event. Don't approach intercourse as an individual pass—fail test. Intercourse is a sharing of pleasure and eroticism.

Second, use multiple stimulation during intercourse rather than depending solely on thrusting. This guideline is especially valuable as individuals and relationships age. Sexuality is an active process—what was easy in the past becomes problematic unless you put new energy into couple sexuality. Couples who value multiple stimulation with sensual, playful, and erotic touch value multiple stimulation during intercourse.

The most common forms of receiving multiple stimulation during intercourse for women are clitoral stimulation (with his fingers, her fingers, or vibrator), buttock or anal stimulation, and breast stimulation. For males, it is receiving testicle stimulation, buttock stimulation, and kissing. For both women and men, the most common type of multiple stimulation is private erotic fantasies. The healthy role of erotic fantasies is as a bridge to desire and a bridge to erotic flow and orgasm. Erotic fantasy works best when it is a private fantasy accepted as such rather than enacting it as a real-life experience. When erotic fantasies are played out they often result in a "sexual dud" (Leitenberg & Henning, 1995). When verbally shared, it feels awkward and increases self-consciousness, which is anti-erotic.

Try these guidelines. Do they enhance your intercourse experience? Do they enhance pleasure and satisfaction for you, your partner, and your relationship?

## Summary

Expand the range of sexuality to include sensual, playful, and erotic touch in addition to intercourse. Emphasize the importance of subjective arousal and that pleasure is more important than performance. Couple sexuality has a range of roles, meanings, and outcomes. You deserve to experience sexuality as shared pleasure rather than a pass—fail individual performance test. By its nature couple sexuality is variable and flexible. Couple sexuality focuses on acceptance and satisfaction; it is anti-perfectionistic. The five dimensions of touch facilitate the sexual mantra of desire/pleasure/eroticism/satisfaction. The most important factor is desire, which is reinforced by anticipation, deserving, freedom, choice, and unpredictable scenarios and techniques. The essence of healthy couple sexuality is giving and receiving pleasure-oriented affectionate, sensual, playful, erotic, and intercourse touch.

# 6

# GOOD ENOUGH SEX (GES)

In male sexual socialization, the media, and movies, the message is that "normal" sex involves totally predictable erection, intercourse, and orgasm (including female orgasm during intercourse). For real-life couples, the Good Enough Sex (GES) model is much superior to this individual perfect performance model in facilitating sexual acceptance and satisfaction (Metz & McCarthy, 2012). By its nature couple sexuality is anti-perfectionism. GES recognizes the multiple roles, meanings, and outcomes of sexuality.

People misinterpret GES as settling for mediocre or routine sex. Nothing can be farther from the truth. GES is a couple concept focused on giving and receiving pleasure. Traditionally, sex had been defined as intercourse. Sex was an individual pass—fail performance centered on intercourse and orgasm. GES recognizes the complexity of sexual roles, meanings, and outcomes. At its core sexuality is a couple process, not an individual performance. GES acknowledges desire/pleasure/eroticism/satisfaction. Adopting GES enhances individual and couple satisfaction. Satisfaction involves much more than intercourse and orgasm.

There are two key issues with GES. First, GES is a couple concept rather than individual performance. Second, the emphasis on variable, flexible sexual response rather than perfect performance. GES supports arousal, intercourse, and orgasm as a healthy part of your sexual experience. The problem occurs when sex function is viewed as a pass—fail test. This increases anticipatory and performance anxiety. GES emphasizes sexuality in context, especially the quality of your relationship (Impett, Peplau & Gable, 2005). A major factor is maintaining positive, realistic sexual expectations. Ideally, a sexual experience is mutual and synchronous. This means that both partners experience desire/pleasure/eroticism/satisfaction. However, among happily married, sexually functional couples less than 50% of sexual encounters are mutual and synchronous. Most sexual encounters are positive yet asynchronous, meaning sex is better for one partner than the other (Frank, Anderson & Rubinstein, 1978). GES celebrates both synchronous and asynchronous sexual experiences. A major source of couple conflict is the performance expectation that both partners must have the same experience, especially orgasm. GES accepts a range of sexual outcomes, including variability and flexibility in desire, arousal, orgasm (with the unrealistic goal of simultaneous orgasm).

GES recognizes that you are an intimate sexual team who accept dynamite sexual encounters, good sex, better than average sex, average sex, dissatisfying sex, and dysfunctional sex. A key concept is that whatever the experience, turn toward your partner as your intimate and erotic friend. Do not engage in blaming or shaming when there is a sexual problem.

GES promotes positive, realistic sexual expectations. Few couples have the ideal sexual experience depicted in movies or romantic novels. Hopefully, 85–95% of experiences are positive. However, the reality is that 5–15% of sexual encounters are dissatisfying or dysfunctional. Even for the most loving, sexually functional couples there is a negative or dissatisfying experience on occasion (even once a month). GES recognizes that couple sexuality is inherently variable and flexible. This reality is denied by the traditional perfect individual performance model.

The most difficult GES concept to accept is asynchronous sexual experiences. Is it okay if one partner has a better sexual time? Yes, and these differences are good for your relationship. The caveat is that asynchronous sex cannot be at the expense of your partner or relationship. This results in power struggles, blaming, and alienation.

Asynchronous sex is usually enjoyable for the other partner. For example, if the man is orgasmic and the woman is not, the experience may still be positive for her. A particularly valuable learning is when the non-orgasmic partner finds the sexual encounter more satisfying than the orgasmic partner. Another example is the woman has an erotic (including orgasm) experience while the man experiences low levels of subjective arousal. In this asynchronous experience, she enjoys sex more, but not at his expense. Another example is the man experiences ejaculatory inhibition (he wants to reach orgasm but cannot establish an erotic flow) while she finds the encounter pleasurable. It's in both partners' best interest to accept asynchronous experiences rather than the man labeling himself dysfunctional or the woman feeling she is a second-class sexual partner.

The most common scenario, especially for couples under 40, is the man reports higher desire with predictable erection and orgasm. The woman's sexual desire and response is variable and flexible, but is healthy and first class. Rather than falling into the traditional male—female intercourse power struggle, the GES approach advocates acceptance of differences in desire without demonizing either the lower desire partner (traditionally the woman) or the higher desire partner. They turn toward each other and reinforce being an intimate sexual team. The key concept is genuine, pleasurable connection. Rather than intercourse or nothing, they are aware of the five dimensions of touch—affection, sensual, playful, erotic, and intercourse. Each partner can initiate, and each has the right to veto (trusting your partner will honor your veto). As an intimate team, you confront unhealthy behaviors such as coercion on one extreme and avoidance on the other extreme. You welcome asynchronous sexual experiences in addition to mutual, synchronous sex. GES recognizes that sexuality is much more than intercourse. Pleasure and consent is the foundation of healthy couple sexuality. Examples of positive asynchronous sexual encounters include holding your partner as she stimulates herself to orgasm, your partner pleasuring you to orgasm, a sexual encounter where he was orgasmic and she wasn't, but she found the experience more satisfying, one partner enjoying a playful sexual encounter while the other found it okay. Asynchronous sexuality adds to sexual variety, pleasure, and satisfaction.

GES affirms the energizing value of mutual, synchronous sexual experiences as special and energizing. This includes dramatic, lustful, dynamite experiences. GES recognizes that this is special, but not the norm. Couples feel disappointed and frustrated because their sex was not exceptional and dramatic. GES accepts a range of sexual experiences from wonderful to good to mediocre. Expecting that all sex should be wonderful sets you up for disappointment. A special strength of GES is realistic expectations. GES will not succeed as a romantic novel or porn video, but motivates real-life couples experiencing real-life sexuality (Metz & McCarthy, 2010).

GES emphasizes the role of sex to energize your bond and reinforce feelings of desire and satisfaction. GES is positive and realistic in affirming both synchronous and asynchronous experiences, although preferring mutual, synchronous sex. A noteworthy value of GES is acceptance of the normality of mediocre, dissatisfying, and dysfunctional sexual experiences. Acceptance does not mean settling for mediocre sex. Acceptance means affirming that couple sexuality is variable, flexible, and complex. Acceptance means not overreacting to experiences which are not positive nor energizing. Turn toward your partner without fear of punishment or rejection. Acceptance is a core component of a secure sexual bond.

"Dynamite" sex is celebrated, but not demanded. GES acknowledges the value of wonderful sex without making it a performance expectation. Healthy couple sexuality is based on acceptance. You make requests and positively influence each other to enhance desire/pleasure/eroticism/satisfaction. When there are different preferences for sexual scenarios and techniques, do not engage in coercion, demands, or threats. Accept that often a scenario or technique is more pleasurable or erotic for one partner than the other. GES does not allow your relationship to be controlled by the "tyranny of mutuality". Mutual scenarios and techniques are ideal, but much of the time your experience is not the same as your partner's. Accept sensual, playful, and erotic differences. You are not clones of each other. Couple sexuality is enhanced by differences and unpredictability. Empathy, intimacy, and nondemand pleasuring provides a base for sexual playfulness, individuality, and flexibility.

## Evan and Angelina

Like many couples of their generation, 33-year-old Evan and 34-year-old Angelina were sexually disappointed. They had special memories of their 14-month limerance phase and thought of themselves as a good sexual couple. However, over the past three years, relational and sexual satisfaction was lower. Evan blamed this on Angelina and her inability to balance her 30-hour a week job and parenting their 3-year-old daughter. Angelina was quite vocal in blaming Evan for being overly focused on his 50-hour a week career and not being an equal parent.

Sex had settled into a late night, weekend routine which was functional for Evan, but not Angelina. Angelina liked the idea of a couple dialogue and adopting GES. She was tired of being blamed by Evan and blaming him. Evan wanted sex to be mutual and synchronous and spent a great deal of time on foreplay, especially cunnilingus, so Angelina would have an orgasm during intercourse. When she was not orgasmic, Evan was very disappointed. Angelina felt her orgasm was more for Evan than for her. Foreplay was more of a task than a pleasure. Eventually she fell into a pattern of "faking orgasm" to placate Evan. They were no longer sexual friends, which reduced relational satisfaction. Evan felt Angelina put inordinate pressure on him to be the "perfect spouse" and "perfect lover". Angelina felt Evan was not the man she had married, but rather a demanding partner.

Angelina and Evan were suffering under the pressure to be a perfect sexual couple controlled by the need for each sexual experience to be mutual, synchronous, and orgasmic. That is not the reality of marriage or couple sex. When they first heard about GES they were not enthusiastic, especially Evan, who feared he would be blamed and there would be little sex—a double loser. Angelina made a wise decision to not pressure Evan to accept GES. Instead, she disclosed her feelings about what had happened to them sexually and her interest in developing a new couple sexuality. Angelina liked having a couple dialogue and that GES was a couple concept. She apologized for faking orgasm. Angelina wanted Evan to understand that her orgasmic pattern (as is true for most of the women she knew) was not the same as his. Trying to act like it was resulted in a sexual turn-off for her. Even at the height of the limerance phase, Angelina's orgasmic response was variable and flexible. She could be orgasmic both before and during intercourse, but not 100% of the time. Angelina's friend who was a PhD sociology researcher told her that among sexually satisfied women the average frequency of orgasm during couple sex was 70%. This was new information for Evan and reduced pressure to "give her an orgasm". Angelina wanted Evan to accept her sexual response pattern as the right fit for her. The more Angelina read and talked with female friends, the better she felt about GES. Acceptance of couple variability and flexibility is a base of GES. This fit Angelina's lived sexual experiences. What Evan expected in terms of orgasmic performance was not the real Angelina.

She valued eroticism and orgasm, but wanted Evan to understand that sensuality and sexual playfulness were important. She could create her erotic scenarios rather than just reacting to his erotic preferences. This was a new perspective for Evan.

Evan's desire to be a good lover was appreciated. Angelina was becoming comfortable with a new sexual language to establish an intimate and erotic friendship with Evan. Angelina now trusted him and felt he was her intimate ally. Angelina had felt de-eroticized by Evan's approach to sex initiation, performance, and orgasm.

The miscommunication was Angelina felt Evan had de-eroticized her because she wasn't "good enough" sexually. Instead of reacting defensively, Evan realized that unintentionally they had de-eroticized each other and their relationship.

Evan's parents had not been a good marital or sexual model. His parents had a stable, but unsatisfying marriage. Evan found it hard to believe they were a sexual couple. Angelina told Evan she had spoken with his mother who told Angelina that sex was a strength of their difficult marriage. Angelina asked Evan whether he was committed to a satisfying, secure, and sexual marriage. This is what she wanted. Could Angelina depend on Evan as her intimate and erotic ally? These were new concepts and language for Evan, and he enthusiastically embraced this. The challenge for Evan was not intentionality, but behavioral follow through. Could he accept Angelina's pleasure and orgasm pattern and not compare it to his? Evan enjoys spontaneous erections and predictable intercourse. He thought of GES as something that couples used in their 60s, not younger couples like he and Angelina.

Abstract arguments and power struggles have no value for the man, woman, or couple. What made the difference for Evan and Angelina was engaging in GES psychosexual skill exercises. Evan initiated two sensual exercises/scenarios and Angelina initiated two erotic exercises/scenarios (one to orgasm and one with a prohibition on orgasm). The sensual experiences were exactly what they hoped for—involving, enjoyable, and bonding. This was particularly motivating for Evan, who realized that GES would add to couple sexuality, not inhibit sexual expression.

The erotic exercises/scenarios were more challenging. Evan wanted Angelina to accept his erection rather than view it as a sign of pressure, but the prohibition on orgasm was not acceptable to him. Evan stimulated himself to orgasm, which previously Angelina had not been comfortable with, feeling intimidated and blamed. Angelina felt highly aroused and enjoyed orgasm with manual and oral stimulation in the first erotic scenario. However, although Evan was easily orgasmic, he was frustrated that it wasn't inside her. Erotic sexual expression was better for Angelina than Evan. The question was whether they could integrate asynchronous erotic scenarios into their couple sexual style. Was it okay that erotic sex was better for Angelina? Rather than being "socially desirable", Evan was able to affirm asynchronous eroticism because it reduced her perceived pressure from his erection. Also, Evan realized this aspect of GES would serve him well as he and their relationship aged. For Angelina, Evan's sexual acceptance and generosity enhanced relational and sexual satisfaction. Not only had they broken the frustrating, demoralizing sexual pattern, but GES concepts and exercises established an openness to the range of sexual roles, meanings, and outcomes. This would serve them well for the next 40 years. Their marriage was on solid footing to remain satisfying, secure, and sexual.

## Major Obstacles for Acceptance of GES

Sex educators and therapists are frustrated that GES has not been widely accepted by couples or the media. GES is just not "sexy". What the media and public want is a simple, "hot", dramatic, and free approach to sex with guaranteed ecstasy. Obviously, this is the opposite of GES.

The major sexual issue is desire. Few people (women or men) report primary low desire. Secondary desire problems are the most common sexual issue for couples. A prime cause is feeling controlled by the perfect intercourse and orgasm performance model. The best example is men with ED. He avoids sex because of fear of erectile failure. Couples are surprised to learn that in the overwhelming majority of cases it is the man's choice to stop sex, especially with aging. When sex is viewed as an individual pass—fail test it sets the stage to give up on sexuality (McCarthy & Pierpaoli, 2015). GES is not dramatic, but it is the answer to enjoying sexuality in your 60s, 70s, and 80s. GES reflects the importance of making wise sexual decisions rather than being governed by the seductive model of perfect sex. This performance model burdens sexual desire for the man, woman, and couple. GES emphasizes that desire and satisfaction is more important than intercourse and orgasm.

A major barrier to acceptance of GES is the male—female sex power struggle. GES is more acceptable for women because it is congruent with her sexual socialization and lived experiences. Variable, flexible female and couple sexuality with a range of meanings and outcomes is congruent with her sexual experiences. The totally predictable sex performance with no variation in quality or meaning is not her sexual experience, much less ideal sex. The vulnerability for the woman is to be blaming and discouraged. The vulnerability for the man is feeling he must sacrifice his right to "real sex". The challenge for the couple is to be intimate and erotic friends; this promotes acceptance of GES. The challenge for the man is to make a "wise" decision and realize that in the long run GES will be good for him, her, and them. Men particularly like the idea that they "beat the odds" and enjoy sexuality in their 60s, 70s, and 80s. The challenge for the woman is to turn toward him in an accepting manner rather than resentfully turn away. She values pleasure-oriented touching personally and as a couple. Women enjoy GES more than the traditional approach to totally predictable intercourse.

The key for breaking the power struggle is sharing pleasure whether or not it transitions to intercourse and orgasm. When the couple become stuck in a "right—wrong" argument everyone loses. When you focus on intimacy, pleasuring, and turning toward each other the power struggle melts away. An advantage of using the new mantra of desire/pleasure/eroticism/satisfaction is the focus on a common language with an emphasis on pleasure. Rather than the traditional gender split, both partners value intimacy, pleasure, and eroticism.

Another barrier involves the role and meaning of eroticism. Traditionally, eroticism was a male concept focused on "intense, lustful, out of control, dramatic sex". The best example is porn videos which portray the male fantasy of the crazy woman turned on by being submissive during painful, degrading sex. That is not congruent with GES.

Remember, the best sex is mutual and synchronous. In addition, asynchronous sex is highly valued. An example is an asynchronous erotic scenario which is better for one partner (usually, but not always) the man. The difference from porn scenarios is the erotic charge is not at the expense of your partner. Integrated eroticism is the opposite of the partner being submissive, crazy, or taken advantage of. Eroticism encourages partners to be swept away with feelings and sensations in a manner which is good for you and your relationship. Integrated eroticism is healthy for the woman, man, and couple. Accepting differences in erotic feelings and scenarios is integral to GES.

Another barrier to acceptance of GES is the perceived need for mutuality in all sexual encounters. Although mutual sex is ideal, believing that all sex must be mutual is untrue and destructive. This results in the "tyranny of mutuality". GES recognizes that you are not sexual clones. Celebrate your sexual voice (autonomy). This adds spice and diversity to couple sexuality. GES recognizes the value of diverse sexual scenarios. Be aware that the same sexual encounter can have a different role, meaning, and outcome for your partner than it has for you. Couple sexuality celebrates sexual differences and variability. It's all part of the complexity of couple sexuality.

A final example of a barrier to GES is the romantic love myth. The romantic love approach believes all sexual encounters should be romantic, loving, and special. We are in favor of romantic feelings, love, and intimacy. The problem occurs when this becomes a demand and negates other motivations for sex and diverse sexual experiences. Sex can be for fun, tension release, sensual pleasure, selfish feelings, orgasm, a way to reconnect, or to spice up a boring routine. Sometimes what you need is a loving, intimate experience, sometimes you need an orgasm. GES affirms real life couple sexuality with its multiple motivations and outcomes rather than expecting all sex to be loving and romantic. It is especially important to affirm sex as a tension reducer to deal with the stresses of a shared life. GES emphasizes accepting a range of sexual outcomes, as well as a range of motivations and meanings.

## Exercise: Accepting GES Outcomes

Begin this exercise by discussing your experiences with dynamite sex, bonding sex, good sex, mediocre sex, and dysfunctional sex. Are you able to accept the entire range of sexual outcomes or do some experiences cause discomfort, embarrassment, or blaming? Some couples find dynamite sex encounters intimidating rather than celebrating these sexual experiences. More commonly, partners feel embarrassed or guilty about dissatisfying or dysfunctional sex. The message of this exercise is acceptance of the normal variability of couple sexuality. You can learn from the past, but cannot change it. Your power for change is in the present and future. This is the challenge for the second part of this exercise.

During the next six months it is highly likely you will have at least one special sexual experience, one good sexual experience, and one dissatisfying or dysfunctional sexual experience. Talk about how you will handle this when it occurs and then implement your coping strategy.

The challenge for the special experience is to genuinely embrace feelings and sensations. You deserve to celebrate a special sexual encounter. Give yourself permission to embrace dynamite sexuality, allow it to energize your bond, and reinforce feelings of sexual desirability and anticipation. Not all sexual encounters can or should be special, but enjoy those that are.

Couples find acceptance of good sexual encounters to be a challenge. Is it okay to have a B-sexual experience? Yes. Sometimes okay is what it is, and you and your partner can accept this. It was worthwhile to be together sexually; no apologies are necessary.

Acceptance of yourself, your partner, and your relationship is the best response to good/okay experiences. Spending time with afterplay to reinforce intimacy can be particularly meaningful after an okay sexual encounter.

For GES the most challenging issue is dealing with dissatisfying or dysfunctional sexual experiences. The key is to turn toward each other as intimate and erotic friends. No need for blame or guilt, you are there for each other in good and bad sexual times.

The worst time to talk sex is when you are nude, lying down, after a negative sexual experience. Partners feel vulnerable and say and do things they regret. The next morning they apologize, but the harm is done. We suggest discussing the negative sexual experience the next day, dressed, on a walk or over a cup of coffee. Is there a message to the experience that needs to be processed? The most common message is you rushed or tried to force sex rather than take your time and focus on pleasure. Most of the time, there is no message other than this is a normal sexual "blip".

Turn toward each other and share intimate, nondemand touch. Dissatisfying or dysfunctional sex need not be a big deal—nothing bad will come from it. Don't be embarrassed or avoidant, make time to talk the next day to ensure you stay on the same intimate sexual team.

Discussing coping strategies is very important, but the most important challenge is to implement this in your couple sexual style. Sexuality involves cognitions, behaviors, and emotional factors. The focus of this exercise is to reinforce being intimate and erotic friends whether the sexual experience was special, good, or dysfunctional. Remember, your power for change is to implement these GES coping strategies in the present and future.

**Summary**

Good Enough Sex (GES) is one of the major breakthroughs in the last 50 years of sex research and clinical practice. Previously, sex function and dysfunction was an individual performance measure which you either passed or failed. This traditional approach is directly confronted by the GES model. By its nature couple sexuality is complex—with a range of roles, meanings, and outcomes. The most important GES concept is that sexuality is a couple process of sharing pleasure, not an individual performance. GES is meant to be inclusive, realistic, and motivating, not a pass—fail individual test. Sex educators and therapists (especially females) are positive about GES, although it is still not widely accepted in the media or by physicians. Partly, this is because of the traditional male performance approach. GES asks both partners to accept vulnerabilities and embrace variable, flexible couple sexuality as the norm. That requires personal courage and openness with your partner.

Sex therapists advocate for acceptance of GES. Does that motivate and empower couples? Usually yes, but not always. It is most acceptable to couples over 50, to women, to those who have experienced sexual problems, and to well-bonded couples. GES is most challenging for young couples, for men, couples in sexual power-struggles, and high conflict couples. GES asks you to be self-accepting, accepting of your partner, and accepting of the complexity of couple sexuality. Variable, flexible couple sexuality sounds like a simple concept, but it entails a wide range of sexual scenarios, techniques, and outcomes. Traditional couples fear that GES will confuse and demoralize them. In fact, GES is an affirmative concept; there is no reason to apologize for GES.

We suggest adopting GES as early as possible. You don't need to wait until you are 50, 60 or until you experience sexual dysfunction. Ideally learn GES in your 20s or 30s. Accept GES experiences as normal variations, not a sex problem.

Be aware of your healthy and unhealthy learnings and experiences about individual sex performance. Share these with your partner. Remember, your power for change is in the present and future. So, what is your decision about GES? Is it the right fit for you personally and relationally? If so, what can you do to implement GES in your life and relationship? GES allows sexuality to have a positive 15–20% role in your life and relationship.

# 7
# INTEGRATING INTIMACY AND EROTICISM

Intimacy and eroticism are very different dimensions. Both are valuable for women, men, and couples. A crucial factor in couple sexuality is to confront the traditional power struggle where men value eroticism and women value intimacy. The new sexual mantra is desire/pleasure/eroticism/satisfaction. This requires the couple to be intimate and erotic friends. After the romantic love/passionate sex (limerance) phase, the challenge for couples, whether married or partnered, straight or gay, is to integrate intimacy and eroticism into your couple sexual style (McCarthy & McCarthy, 2014).

Intimacy and eroticism are different, but not adversarial or incompatible. Intimacy involves warm, loving, affectionate, sensual, pleasure-oriented, predictable feelings which reinforce attachment. Eroticism involves intense sensations and feelings, mystery and creativity, taking emotional and sexual risks, unpredictability, fantasies which are not socially acceptable, and vitality. The challenge for the man is to develop his "intimate voice" and value pleasure-oriented touch. The challenge for the woman is to find her "erotic voice" and value vital sexuality.

A common clinical dilemma is the woman who says "I love my spouse, but am not in love with him". The man complains she was a great premarital partner, but "marriage kills sex". Sadly, these gender stereotypic complaints become a self-fulfilling prophecy. Couples fall into the trap of eroticism as the man's domain and intimacy the woman's domain. This is destructive for the man, woman, couple, and the culture. It forms the basis for the traditional power struggle of "intercourse or nothing".

When both partners value intimacy and eroticism, sexuality is an intimate team experience. Intimacy is not instead of intercourse nor the enemy of eroticism. Valuing desire/pleasure/eroticism/satisfaction is the foundation for couple sexuality. Both partners valuing intimacy facilitates an integrated approach to couple sexuality. In the same manner, eroticism is a joint domain. Eroticism is integrated in the sexual relationship rather than separate from it. Porn scenarios feature eroticism separated from intimacy. The challenge is to value integrated eroticism which is part of the intimacy, pleasure, and sexuality experience, not separate from it. Too many men view eroticism as a male performance. The porn model emphasizes that the crazier the woman the more erotic she is. In contrast, integrated eroticism is healthy for the woman, man, couple, and culture.

## The Role of Intimacy

Intimacy facilitates pleasuring. It is neither necessary nor sufficient for sex, but intimacy promotes genuine couple bonding. Intimacy is a bridge to sexual desire and enhances satisfaction. Intimacy involves both emotional and physical components. Emotionally you feel a genuine openness and secure attachment. He is responsive to your needs and feelings. You believe "my spouse has my back". Intimacy allows you to feel safe and connected. Emotional intimacy nurtures your couple bond while sexual intimacy energizes the bond. Emotional and sexual intimacy are different dimensions, but reinforce each other. Intimacy involves warm, loving, predictable feelings of attachment and security. When couples divorce (or break-up) it is a major loss because of broken intimacy. You share greater intimacy with your spouse (life partner) than in any other relationship. The integration of emotional and sexual intimacy is special and empowering.

## The Role of Eroticism

The essence of eroticism is intense emotions and sensations. It is this intensity which makes eroticism more controversial than intimacy. Eroticism involves creativity and mystery, unpredictability, non-socially acceptable fantasies, taking emotional and sexual risks, and erotic playfulness. Eroticism is energizing and intensifies sexual desire. In terms of subjective pleasure, eroticism involves feelings/sensations from "6–10". Objective arousal/eroticism involves lubrication, erection, and orgasm.

Eroticism is an integral component in the desire/pleasure/eroticism/satisfaction mantra. Eroticism is integral for the woman, man, and couple. Integrated eroticism is totally different than the porn model or dramatic lust portrayed in videos. Eroticism is not a sex performance, a manipulation, proving yourself sexually, or impressing your partner. Own your eroticism and share your sexual self with your partner. Orgasm is an integral part of eroticism, not a pass—fail performance test. You share pleasure, arousal, erotic flow, and orgasm. Eroticism involves giving and receiving manual, oral, and rubbing stimulation. Orgasm is the natural continuation of the pleasuring/eroticism process where high arousal flows to orgasm.

## Erotic Fantasies

The most common erotic stimulus is sexual fantasies. Erotic fantasies are an example of the creativity and non-socially acceptable component of eroticism. No one fantasizes about intercourse in the missionary position with their spouse in their bedroom. What makes a fantasy erotic is that it is different than your real-life behavior. Common erotic fantasies include being sexual with a person you're not supposed to be sexual with, group or triadic sex, forced or being forced sexually, watching others being sexual or them watching you, being sexual with someone of the same gender. The key to enjoying erotic fantasy is awareness that fantasy is very different than real-life sexuality. Sexual fantasies do not mean this is what you want sexually. Fantasy is erotically charged because it breaks boundaries and is illicit. Erotic fantasies serve as a bridge for sexual desire and as an erotic charge to orgasm. Non-socially acceptable erotic fantasies are normal and healthy. Erotic fantasies become self-defeating when they are perceived as shameful, used in a narrow or compulsive manner, or you confuse fantasy and reality. Enjoy your erotic fantasies without fear or shame. Use erotic fantasies for multiple stimulation, including during intercourse.

## The Couple Challenge: Integrating Intimacy and Eroticism

Most couples begin their relationship in the limerance phase (romantic love/passionate sex/idealization). Intimacy and eroticism flow in a special, unselfconscious manner. Unfortunately, limerance is a fragile, time-limited experience, lasting between six months and two years. The challenge for couples whether married or partnered, straight or gay, is to develop a couple sexual style which facilitates strong, resilient sexual desire by integrating intimacy and eroticism. The most common couple sexual style is Complementary, where each partner values intimacy and eroticism. Other couple sexual styles deal differently with intimacy and eroticism (McCarthy & McCarthy, 2009). The Traditional sexual style splits gender roles where the man values eroticism and the woman intimacy. The Best Friend sexual style emphasizes intimacy and downplays eroticism. In contrast, the Emotionally Expressive sexual style values eroticism and downplays intimacy.

What is the best way for you to integrate intimacy and eroticism into your relationship? The Complementary couple sexual style is the best fit for most couples. Choose the couple sexual style which is the best fit for you. Recognize that both intimacy and eroticism are important for couple sexuality.

## Nate and Trini

Nate and Trini met the year after college graduation. Nate was in a management training program. He firmly believed in a traditional life organization and traditional gender roles. Trini advocated for women's rights and was dedicated to her career as a print artist. She enjoyed planning couple activities, especially going to clubs, listening to music, and attending afternoon artistic events. She was pleased that Nate was willing to pay for these activities. He was comfortable with the tradition that the man paid for meals and events, although if Trini insisted he was flexible about her picking up the tab.

Trini found it interesting that her parents were fond of Nate, more than any man she had introduced to them. They had unsuccessfully tried to talk Trini out of her career decisions, worried she would not be able to support herself as a print artist. As a traditional man, Nate would financially support her and Trini could be a wife, mother, and part-time print artist. However, Trini wanted a different life organization. Nate respecting Trini's independence and artistic work was crucial. Trini and Nate were a romantic love/passionate sex couple, but Trini did not idealize Nate and didn't want to be idealized by him.

When couples are considering marriage or life partnership, they need to discuss both emotional and practical issues. Love is important, but it is not enough for a satisfying, secure, and sexual relationship. Trini and Nate discussed practical issues of money, children, and where to live. Even more important were disclosing their psychological, relational, and sexual strengths and vulnerabilities; how to integrate intimacy and eroticism; whether they would have a traditional monogamy commitment or consensual non-monogamy; and how to deal with differences and conflicts.

A crucial issue was to develop a couple sexual style which integrated intimacy and eroticism. Nate wanted to keep eroticism, including intercourse initiation and frequency, as his domain. He wanted sex to be good for Trini, but believed in the double standard and felt that the Traditional sexual style was the right fit for him. However, it was not the right fit for Trini. The double standard meant she had to give up her erotic initiations and preferences. The core conflict was about the role and meaning of "foreplay". Nate enjoyed his spontaneous erections and providing genital stimulation for Trini. Nate felt he was a patient, giving partner, but Trini didn't appreciate what a good lover he was. They talked about sex when they were being sexual as well as a "post-game" analysis after sex.

Talk about sexuality in an open, personally meaningful way. Unfortunately, the way Nate and Trini talked about sex was counter-productive, increasing defensiveness and self-consciousness.

The best time to talk about sexuality is either the day before a sexual encounter or in a therapist's office. The best way to talk about sexuality is to begin by saying what you value about your partner and your sexual relationship (be sure you are genuine, not being "socially desirable"). Then make requests about the scenarios and techniques you want to experiment with the next time you are sexual. Acceptance is the foundation for the change process. Put-downs, complaining, and demands elicit defensiveness and counter attacks. Change is motivating when based on acceptance of your partner and desire to enhance couple sexuality.

The key is requests, not demands. A request says you own your feelings, want to experiment with something different, and ask your partner to be your intimate and erotic ally in exploring whether a new scenario or technique enhances individual and couple sexuality. A demand says you need to do this to prove you love me, do it my way, and if it fails I will blame you and there will be negative consequences. Demands treat sex as a transaction and performance test. Requests invite you to be intimate and erotic allies. Demands are about performance with the threat of negative consequences.

Trini wanted to talk about sexuality outside of the bedroom, preferably over a glass of wine, sitting on the porch. She needed Nate to see her as his equitable sexual partner who valued both intimacy and eroticism. Trini wanted to break out of the rigid gender roles and establish a new couple sexual style where intimacy and eroticism joined them rather than split them.

This dialogue was valuable for Nate. He was afraid Trini had an agenda to underplay eroticism and intercourse frequency. Understanding that Trini valued receiving pleasurable and erotic touch was important. However, the traditional foreplay scenario where he was active and she passive did not work for her. It had been inviting during the limerance phase, but now it made her feel self-conscious, which was anti-erotic. Nate's sexual intentions were good, but the outcome was the opposite of what he wanted.

Trini's request was to replace the foreplay scenario with an active, giving and receiving pleasure-oriented scenario. This would be challenging, but Trini and Nate would succeed if they approached sexuality as intimate and erotic allies. Trini wanted to be an active, first-class woman, including maintaining her "erotic voice". Her eroticism was not a threat to Nate. This facilitates sharing couple eroticism. The challenge for

Nate was to value pleasuring for himself rather than to prepare her for intercourse. Nate's fear that intimate, pleasure-oriented touch would somehow rob him of confident male sex was just that—an irrational fear. Male sexuality is enhanced by female sexuality, not diminished by it. Male sexuality values intimacy and pleasuring in addition to eroticism and intercourse. This was an opportunity for Nate to learn a broad-based sexuality which would serve him well throughout his life. Nate loved the concept of being a "wise" man who could enjoy intimacy, pleasuring, and eroticism in his 60s, 70s, and 80s. Trini's respect and love for Nate grew. She realized he was open to her positive influence and that his enthusiasm for eroticism and sexuality had a positive influence on her. They were intimate and erotic allies in a way which reinforced vital, satisfying couple sexuality.

## The Core Challenge of Intimacy and Eroticism

As a culture and in sexual socialization, the message is that intimacy and eroticism are separate dimensions and naturally are split. The most common sexual split is by gender, but other sources of splits include casual sex vs. loving sex, hook-up sex vs. relational sex, performance sex vs. pleasurable sex, crazy sex vs. spiritual sex, new relationship sex vs. ongoing relationship sex, bad sex vs. good sex. The traditional message is clear—intimacy and eroticism do not belong together. Our message is very different. Intimacy and eroticism are vital for sexual desire and satisfaction. This is not only necessary, but enhances the sexual experience for the woman, man, and couple. Confront the splits whether based on gender or other dimensions. Value integrated couple sexuality. The preferred integration is that both partners value intimacy and eroticism. The core issue is to ensure that both intimacy and eroticism exist in your relationship. Sex without eroticism is either bland or dysfunctional. Sex without intimacy is a performance which can result in alienation. The most human, genuine, and satisfying sexuality integrates intimacy and eroticism.

Good words and good intentions are not enough. In fact, this fosters disappointment and blaming when not successfully implemented. The core of healthy couple sexuality is genuine attitudinal, behavioral, emotional enactment to promote change. Change does not mean being perfect. It means genuine experiences of high levels of intimacy and eroticism. It means breaking the cycle of competitiveness between intimacy and eroticism, emphasizing acceptance of touch. For many couples, nongenital massage expresses your sense of sensuality. For others, it involves a combination of seductive and playful touch. Others emphasize erotic touch to energize your bond.

The following psychosexual skill exercises are to make personal and concrete these challenges. There is not a "perfect" or "right" way to approach intimacy and eroticism. The challenge is to find the best approach for you.

### Exercise One: Valuing Intimacy

Intimacy has both a physical and emotional component. Each partner initiates your preferred intimacy scenario. The crucial factor is that each person's scenario is genuine—your favorite way to initiate and experience intimacy. For some people (not controlled by gender stereotypes) intimacy has a strong verbal component and for others the chief feature of intimacy is physical closeness. Affectionate touch—whether holding hands, hugging, or kissing—is an essential component for intimate feelings. Sensual touching (cuddling, massage, back or head scratch, rhythmic touch, or non-genital stroking) enhances intimacy. For others, intimate touch involves a combination of seductive and playful touch. For many, intimacy is about close, predictable attachment. For others, intimacy is about mystery, playful, and unpredictable touching. Again, this is not a "right" or "wrong" response, but to genuinely express what intimacy means for you. Subjective pleasure/arousal intimacy involves a range of 1–5. In all likelihood, your preferred way to initiate and express intimacy will be different than your partner's. This reinforces that you are not clones. Establish your "intimate voice" and recognize your partner's intimate voice. Many couples will try this exercise two, three, or even four times until both are comfortable sharing intimacy.

### Exercise Two: Valuing Eroticism

Like intimacy, eroticism has an emotional and physical component. Eroticism involves intense emotions and sensations. This does not mean it is more genuine or important. It means that intimacy and eroticism are different dimensions. The core understanding is that although different, intimacy and eroticism are not incompatible or adversarial.

Eroticism can center on verbal expression—creating intense scenarios, using explicit and lustful language, "talking dirty", saying how aroused you feel, wanting him inside you, letting go and "coming", saying it "feels so good", and expressing immense pleasure and satisfaction. Erotic expression involves intense emotions and sensations. Both subjective (feeling "hot") and objective (lubrication, erection, orgasm) responses signal eroticism. Eroticism involves feelings and sensations in the 6–10 range. Many couples transition to intercourse as soon as he's aroused (subjective arousal of 4–5). We suggest transitioning to intercourse when he's into an "erotic flow" of subjective arousal at least a 7 and ideally 8. This enhances eroticism for the woman because it allows her pleasure and arousal to build before intromission. It is valuable for the man's arousal and eroticism to transition to intercourse when he's turned-on rather than as soon as he can. Experiment with when and how to transition to intercourse so it enhances eroticism for you and your partner.

An important suggestion is to engage in multiple stimulation during intercourse rather than depending solely on thrusting. The most common types of receiving for the woman are clitoral stimulation (with his fingers, her fingers, or a vibrator), anal or buttock stimulation, and breast stimulation. The most common types of receiving for the man are testicle stimulation, buttock stimulation, and kissing stimulation. Experiment with giving and receiving multiple stimulation. Does this enhance eroticism for you and your partner? Some prefer single stimulation. Others find erotic response is enhanced by either giving or receiving. Play with different erotic scenarios and see what is inviting and a turn-on for you. Be aware that your erotic preferences are usually different than your partner's. This is normal and healthy, you are not clones. Erotic differences add spice and vitality to your sexual relationship. Over time erotic scenarios and techniques are likely to change. Eroticism is facilitated by unpredictability. Routine, mechanical sex subverts eroticism.

Be sure that the woman's erotic voice is something she owns and is genuine. It is not to perform for the partner nor to turn him on, but to own your turn-ons and eroticism.

## Three Styles of Arousal

There are three major erotic styles—partner interaction arousal, self-entrancement arousal, and role enactment arousal (Mosher, 1980). Partner interaction arousal focuses on giving and receiving sexual touch. Your arousal enhances your partner's. This is the type of arousal seen in movies where an aroused partner is the major aphrodisiac. In self-entrancement arousal, one partner gives pleasure and the other partner is the receiver. They usually take turns. The receiving partner is aware and mindful, not passive; focused on pleasurable and erotic sensations. In role enactment arousal, the focus is on external stimulation to provide an erotic charge. This could include watching an erotic video, using a sex toy like a vibrator, visual feedback from a mirror, or acting out an erotic fantasy.

Most couples utilize partner interaction as their primary source of eroticism. Some couples use all three erotic styles, but most utilize two styles and on special occasions add a third. Self-entrancement arousal becomes more common as couples age.

The question is, what is the most inviting arousal style or styles for you? Talking is important, but the crucial dimension is enacting each arousal style and determining what is the best fit for you individually and as a couple. Being open and comfortable with arousal style(s) is integral to healthy eroticism.

## Exercise Three: Integrating Intimacy and Eroticism

There is not one right way to integrate intimacy and eroticism, but it is crucial to create a successful integration. The most common integration is the Complementary couple sexual style where both partners value intimacy and eroticism. This directly confronts the traditional gender split of women valuing intimacy and men valuing eroticism.

What is the best way to integrate intimacy and eroticism into your relationship? Reading and dialogue is important, but the key is trying out scenarios to ensure that attitudinally, behaviorally, and emotionally intimacy and eroticism are valued parts of your sexual relationship. Traditional sexual style couples are satisfied with experiencing male-dominant eroticism and female-dominant intimacy. For Traditional sexual style couples, we suggest that once every six months the man initiate an intimacy date with a prohibition on intercourse and every six months the woman initiates a playful or erotic date and it is her decision whether to transition to intercourse or not. This recognizes the value of traditional gender roles while putting variability and spice in their Traditional couple sexual style.

For Best Friend sexual style, a suggested strategy is that every six months each partner initiate an asynchronous playful or erotic scenario. The message is that not all sex needs to be intimate and mutual. Valuing erotic sexuality is a special challenge for Best

Friend sexual couples. Typically, they focus on integrated eroticism and partner interaction arousal. Initiating a "selfish" erotic scenario reinforces that each partner has a unique erotic voice.

The challenge for the Emotionally Expressive sexual style is to value intimacy and nondemand pleasuring. This is not to dilute erotic expression, but to add to their sexual relationship by recognizing the value of intimacy and pleasuring. Not all sexual encounters need to be intense and dramatic.

The value of intimacy and eroticism is recognized by each couple sexual style. Each sexual style has its strengths and vulnerabilities. Integrating intimacy and eroticism is a core factor in choosing the couple sexual style which is the right fit for you.

Most couples choose the Complementary sexual style because it fits the equity model of the woman and man valuing intimacy and eroticism. The Complementary sexual style supports both synchronous and asynchronous sexual scenarios as well as his, hers, and their bridges to sexual desire. The challenges for the Complementary sexual style are that it requires dialogue and negotiation, confronts traditional gender roles, and that your relational style is usually different than your sexual style. The Complementary couple sexual style is the most common and a good fit, but not for all couples.

The Traditional sexual style is the easiest to understand and implement. The man values eroticism and intercourse while the woman values intimacy, affection, and relational stability. There is little need for negotiation; both partners understand and play out their traditional relational and sexual roles. The Traditional relational and sexual styles are quite compatible. The vulnerability of the Traditional sexual style is rigid roles which can cause resentment, alienation, and dysfunction.

Couples fall into the Best Friend sexual style because it is compatible with the Best Friend relational style—the most commonly chosen relational style. The Best Friend sexual style emphasizes intimacy, closeness, and mutuality. When it functions well the couple feel securely attached with warm, loving sex. There are two major vulnerabilities with this sexual style. First, there is so much closeness that you de-eroticize your partner. Second, there is so much emphasis on mutuality that you don't take emotional and sexual risks, so there is a lot of together time, but low sex frequency. Be sure you choose this style as the best fit for you rather than assume this is the right way to be sexual. Be sure you are sexual friends, not just intimate friends.

The strength of the Emotionally Expressive sexual style is the emphasis on sexual intensity, vitality, and creating dramatic sexual scenarios. Emotionally Expressive sexual couples have the most fun and are most likely to use role enactment arousal scenarios with sexual games and toys. The vulnerability of this sexual style is too much sexual drama. Sex disrupts your bond by breaking boundaries and draining the relationship. Sexual drama and struggles can subvert the relationship. Do not allow erotic conflicts to subvert intimacy and relational security.

The personal responsibility/intimate sexual team model is challenged when trying to find the right mix of intimacy and eroticism. You are not clones of each other—each partner has their sexual voice. As a sexual team, you find the best fit for integrating intimacy and eroticism. Couples stuck in a sexual power struggle find this is destructive for the woman, man, and couple. Rather than sexuality enhancing and energizing your relationship, the power struggle drains you and your relationship. Find your unique way to value intimacy and eroticism.

## Positive, Realistic Expectations of Intimacy and Eroticism

So much of sex in the media (internet, articles, books, movies) promises "magical", perfect sex. Love and intimacy with your "soul mate" overcomes everything. Dramatic, powerful eroticism carries you to perfect ecstasy. Perfect intimacy and perfect eroticism is fiction; subverting real life couple sexuality.

By its nature couple sexuality is variable, flexible, and complex. Sexuality has several roles, meanings, and outcomes. It is seldom perfect. You are not a sex machine. You are real people with a real relationship. Sometimes intimacy is wonderful and affirming, sometimes predictable and bonding, and other times frustrating and disappointing. Sometimes eroticism is vital and satisfying, sometimes functional and good, and other times a dud or dysfunctional. We affirm the value of intimacy and eroticism while recognizing it can have a range of meanings and outcomes.

Sometimes an encounter is intimate but not erotic and other times lustful and erotic, but the emotion is anger. Intimacy and eroticism are separate dimensions. The best sex integrates intimacy and eroticism. Accept that sexuality has several roles and meanings, and sometimes is different for one partner than the other. Acceptance of variability, flexibility, and complexity is key for healthy couple sexuality.

Intimacy was supposed to be necessary for eroticism, especially for women. In addition, intimacy was more highly valued than eroticism. This hierarchy negates the desire/pleasure/eroticism/satisfaction mantra. There is not a competition or a split. Valuing intimacy and eroticism is healthy for the woman, man, couple, and culture.

# 8

# YOUR COUPLE SEXUAL STYLE

Traditionally, it was assumed that the couple's sexual style would be the same as their relational style. A valuable insight is that for most couples their relational and sexual styles are different. This is motivating and empowering.

Your relational style refers to how you deal with differences and conflicts. This is an excellent predictor for a successful marriage (or life partnership). For most couples, the Best Friend relational style is the best fit. Best Friend couples have differences and conflicts (remember, you are not clones of each other), but these do not degenerate into chronic power struggles. Your relationship involves respect, trust, and emotional intimacy. Your relationship is based on a positive influence process. A crucial factor is you "trust your partner has your back". Even when frustrated, disappointed, or angry you trust your partner would not do something to intentionally hurt you.

The couple sexual style is different than the relational style. Your couple sexual style involves maintaining your sexual voice (autonomy) and at the same time being an intimate sexual team. The second factor is how you integrate intimacy and eroticism in your sexual relationship. The most common couple sexual style is Complementary, although there is not one sexual style that fits all couples.

The Best Friend relational style is the best fit for most couples. However, the Best Friend sexual style is not a good fit for most couples. There is so much emphasis on intimacy (with eroticism downplayed) that you de-eroticize your partner and relationship. Too much intimacy can subvert sexual desire.

The best fit for the majority of couples is the Complementary couple sexual style. Each partner maintains their sexual voice while being an intimate sexual team. Both partners value intimacy and eroticism and recognize the multiple roles, meanings, and outcomes of couple sexuality. The Complementary couple sexual style affirms the value of affectionate, sensual, playful, and erotic touch in addition to intercourse. The Complementary sexual style affirms Good Enough Sex (GES).

## The Four Couple Sexual Styles

The four major couple sexual styles by frequency are:

1. Complementary.
2. Traditional.
3. Best Friend.
4. Emotionally Expressive.

Remember, sexually one size never fits all. The challenge is to discover which couple sexual style is the best fit for you and your relationship. Remember, your couple sexual style is usually not the same as your relational style (McCarthy & Ross, 2017).

### The Complementary Couple Sexual Style

The Complementary sexual style is the most frequently chosen because it reflects the guideline of being responsible for your sexuality and valuing your partner as your intimate and erotic ally. You have your bridges to sexual desire, your partner's bridges to desire, and couple bridges. You value both synchronous and asynchronous sexual experiences. Complementary sexual style couples value sensual, playful, and erotic touch in addition to intercourse. Female—male sexual equity is affirmed in the Complementary sexual style. The concept of Good Enough Sex (GES) which recognizes the multiple roles, meanings, and outcomes of couple sexuality is congruent with the Complementary sexual style.

A major vulnerability of the Complementary couple sexual style is the dialogue and effort it requires to adopt and implement. Complementary couple sexual style is not simple or "natural". It requires thought, energy, focus, and practice to become an integral part of your, your partner's, and your couple approach to sharing desire/pleasure/eroticism/satisfaction. It is a worthwhile challenge, but requires time, thought, and effort to establish and maintain your Complementary couple sexual style.

### The Traditional Couple Sexual Style

This Traditional sexual style is congruent with the traditional gender roles of the double standard. In the Traditional couple sexual style, the man's domain is sexual initiation and intercourse frequency. Intimacy, affection, and relational stability is the woman's domain. A major strength of the Traditional sexual style is both partners understand and accept their sexual role. Also, it feels "natural" that the relational and sexual styles are congruent. These couples advocate for traditional values of marital stability and family. There is little reason to discuss and negotiate about sexual issues since both partners accept that the man and woman have different preferences, feelings, and values. Couples who value predictability and stability affirm the Traditional sexual style.

Two major vulnerabilities of the Traditional couple sexual style are that the roles are too rigid and result in resentment. Second, with aging and illness the man needs the woman's support and stimulation for continued sexual function. To reduce these vulnerabilities the couple are urged to have occasional experiences where the man initiates an intimacy date with a prohibition on intercourse and the woman initiates a playful or erotic date. Respect traditional gender roles, but on occasion spice them up. This includes the man's openness to her pleasuring him rather than demanding he function autonomously.

The Traditional couple sexual style is very compatible with the Traditional relational style. This is the sexual style which is most accepting of decreased sexual frequency with the aging of the couple and their relationship. It is also the most stable couple style, valuing marriage and family.

*Best Friend Couple Sexual Style*

The Best Friend sexual style emphasizes intimacy and mutuality. Sex as an expression of loving feelings is highly valued, as is a secure couple bond. Couples adopt the Best Friend relational style and assume they should adopt a Best Friend sexual style. This can be a self-defeating assumption. It is the norm, not the exception, that the couple relational style and couple sexual style are different. This is especially true for the Best Friend sexual style.

The core vulnerability with the Best Friend sexual style is its emphasis on intimacy at the expense of eroticism. Couples who value the Best Friend sexual style emphasize the benefits of loving, secure feelings and the power of intimacy. Your challenge is to enjoy the benefits of the Best Friend sexual style without sexuality being subverted by common traps. Another vulnerability is you put so much emphasis on mutuality that you do not make sexual initiations or take sexual risks so there is low sexual frequency. You cuddle and hang out, but have little sex.

*Emotionally Expressive Couple Sexual Style*

This is the most fun, erotic, vital sexual style. People envy Emotionally Expressive sexual couples because of sexual intensity and drama. This is the sexual style most likely to utilize role enactment arousal and is the most resilient sexual style.

A vulnerability of the Emotionally Expressive sexual style is breaking emotional and sexual boundaries. Sexual drama can be draining and destabilizing. Another vulnerability is an overemphasis on eroticism and sexual intensity which makes the Emotionally Expressive sexual style the least stable.

If this is your chosen couple sexual style, enjoy the sexually intense emotions and sensations. Embrace the sexual drama and vitality. However, be mindful of boundaries and don't allow sexuality to destabilize you or your relationship.

## Making a Wise Decision

A "wise" decision about your couple sexual style is crucial. Wise means it works both emotionally and practically, in the short and long term. So many couples make no decision or make an "emotional choice" which feels good at the time, but later you regret that choice. It is worth your time and effort to make a wise decision about your couple sexual style. Focus on the 15–20% positive role of sexuality in your life and relationship.

The initial step is to choose the relational style which is the right fit. Relational style involves how you deal with differences and conflicts. For most couples, the best fit is the Best Friend relational style. This relational style reinforces intimacy and security. Couples value a genuine bond and a well-functioning marital (or partnered) relationship. In addition, you are confident "my partner has my back" (Johnson, 2008). Best Friend relational style does not mean that everything is perfect. You accept that there are disappointments and frustrations. You trust that your partner would not do anything to intentionally hurt you. This allows you to dialogue about feelings and problem solve rather than stay stuck in a power struggle. No one wins a power struggle, for it is about who is the "bad person". Power struggles are destructive for the woman, man, and couple. The Best Friend relational style facilitates active involvement as an emotionally intimate team. Choose the relational style which is the best fit for you.

Next, make a wise decision about your couple sexual style. Be aware that usually your couple sexual style is different than your relational style.

Each couple sexual style has its strengths and vulnerabilities. Choose the sexual style which is the best fit for you. This is a crucial couple decision. Sexuality can have a positive, integral role in your life and relationship (McCarthy & McCarthy, 2009).

The Complementary couple sexual style is the most commonly chosen because it is congruent with the model of personal responsibility for desire/pleasure/eroticism/satisfaction while being a well-bonded sexual team. At its core, sexuality is a couple process.

The Complementary sexual style facilitates her, his, and their bridges to sexual desire. It affirms the value of both synchronous and asynchronous couple sexuality. Both partners value intimacy and eroticism. The Complementary sexual style helps you accept GES and the multiple roles, meanings, and outcomes of couple sexuality. The Complementary couple sexual style is the best fit for the majority of (not all) couples.

If you decide on the Complementary sexual style be aware of its vulnerabilities and ensure you do not fall into those traps. The major vulnerability is taking sex for granted and not putting thought and energy into maintaining vital, satisfying couple sexuality. You cannot treat sexuality with benign neglect. Sexual desire is facilitated by anticipation, focus on pleasure, freedom, choice, and unpredictable scenarios and techniques. Taking the Complementary sexual style for granted decreases desire and satisfaction. Another vulnerability is that as life circumstances change (birth of a child, job loss, illness) your Complementary sexual style ignores the changes and loses its special value. Accept changes and integrate them into couple sexuality. Your Complementary sexual style cannot rest on its laurels; sexuality requires dialogue and energy to remain vital and satisfying.

For couples who decide on the Traditional couple sexual style, the advantage is this is congruent with the Traditional relational style and is easily implemented. The relational and sexual norms are accepted by both partners. The assumption is that the man and woman are very different, and their roles are very different. The man is the sexual initiator with a focus on intercourse frequency. The woman's focus is on intimacy, affection, and relational stability. There is no need for discussion and compromise, each knows and accepts the rules of the sex game. Communication is with same gender friends and relatives who make jokes about the opposite gender. Traditional couples value family, relational predictability, and stability. Sex is the man's domain, affection is the woman's domain.

There are two main vulnerabilities for the Traditional couple sexual style. With the aging of the man, his sexual performance becomes less predictable, but he is reluctant to ask for sexual help and stimulation. If he gives up on intercourse, this is the couple sexual style which allows you to accept the no sex state of the marriage (especially if you continue to be an affectionate couple). The second major vulnerability is the roles are so rigid that resentment builds. Typically, the man blames the woman for ending the sexual relationship. Typically, the woman resents that his intercourse focus is at the expense of her need for intimacy and pleasure-oriented touching.

The major strength of the Best Friend couple sexual style is you share intimacy and sexuality with your intimate friend. You have a secure bond and trust your best friend would never cheat on you or hurt you. Your Best Friend sexual style reinforces your Best Friend relational style. You need not fear sexual pressure or coercion. You value mutuality and sharing intimacy. This is the most socially accepted sexual style, especially for women.

There are three major vulnerabilities with the Best Friend sexual style. First, there is so much intimacy and closeness that you de-eroticize the spouse and relationship. Second, there is so much emphasis on mutuality (the "tyranny of mutuality") that you don't take emotional or sexual initiations, so there is low sex frequency. You cuddle and hang out, but unless both of you are desirous you are not sexual. Third, when an affair occurs the Best Friend couple has the hardest time recovering, you stay stuck in feeling betrayed and cannot rebond your marriage. The Best Friend relational style is a much better fit than the Best Friend sexual style.

The Emotionally Expressive couple sexual style is the most dramatic, vital, and experimental. This is the sexual style portrayed in magazines and the one that others envy. Emotionally Expressive sexual couples are most likely to utilize role enactment arousal/eroticism, use sexual toys, play out erotic fantasies, and be sexually resilient after an affair. You pride yourselves in feeling sexually free and experimental. You are more likely to be non-traditional, including embracing consensual non-monogamy.

Two major vulnerabilities of the Emotionally Expressive couple sexual style is that with so much drama you feel drained by the emotional roller coaster. In the heat of conflict boundaries are crossed, causing great damage. A useful guideline is to never argue about sex when nude in bed after a negative sexual experience. Partners say and do things they regret. Even though they apologize the next day the damage has been done. The best time to talk about sexual problems is in a therapist's office or while sitting on the porch or on a walk. Request what you want to try the next time you are sexual. To minimize emotionally draining traps, agree to take a "time-out" before the argument becomes intense and destructive. Remember, sex cannot save a relationship, but sex can destroy a relationship.

## Maura and Dan

Maura and Dan began as a romantic love/passionate sex/idealized (limerance) couple. Dan had never dated a more pro-intercourse woman. Maura was desirous, aroused, and easily orgasmic during intercourse. They had intercourse each time they were together. Dan and Maura began cohabitating with the understanding that this would be a lifetime partnership, but if it did not work (especially sexually) they would not remain a couple. When they decided to marry 18 months later, family and friends were very enthusiastic and supportive. However, what friends did not realize was that the sexual "buzz" was beginning to fizzle. In a reversal of traditional gender roles, it was Maura who complained about Dan's lack of enthusiasm for intercourse. Dan felt attacked and reacted defensively, resulting in a power struggle over intercourse. Each spouse blamed the other. Power struggles are not about a positive agenda. Power struggles are about who is the "bad spouse".

In many ways, Maura and Dan were best friends who admired each other. They easily decided on the Best Friend relational style. Maura assumed that the Best Friend sexual style should naturally follow and that a mutual desire for intercourse would enhance couple sexuality. Dan was anxious and confused about what he wanted sexually for himself and with Maura. He was open to giving manual and oral stimulation before intercourse. During intercourse he enjoyed providing multiple stimulation, especially clitoral and buttock stimulation. However, it was one-way, not reciprocated. Maura felt no need to touch Dan before or during intercourse. In her dating experiences and with Dan she assumed men had easy, totally predictable erections. Older men might have to use Viagra, but Dan at 32 should function autonomously (and should not need anything from her for erection and intercourse).

Maura and Dan were like so many couples. They did not know how to transition from the limerance phase to developing a couple sexual style focused on strong, resilient sexual desire. They became stuck in a destructive power struggle about intercourse.

The essence of a healthy marriage is a respectful, trusting, emotional commitment. Sex is a small (15–20%) integral component which energizes your marital bond and reinforces feelings of desire and desirability. The first task, deciding on the relational style which is the best fit, was easy. Maura and Dan reaffirmed the Best Friend relational style. This was the right fit for their values and goals. The issue of a couple sexual style was much more of a challenge.

Dan valued Maura, was attracted to her, and wanted to share desire/pleasure/eroticism/satisfaction with her. He valued arousal, intercourse, and orgasm. Dan's concern was Maura's belief that all touching had to result in intercourse and that he should be able to perform on demand with no additional stimulation. This caused performance anxiety. Dan wanted to enjoy playful and erotic scenarios in addition to intercourse. He worried that Maura's romantic and sexual expectations were extreme. He enjoyed her being pro-sexual, but not her demand that all sex must be mutual and result in intercourse.

Maura's assumptions were that the Best Friend sexual style should naturally follow their relational style, that all sex should be mutual and perfect, and sex=intercourse (anything else meant there was a problem). As this was articulated, Maura became aware that it sounded more like a demand than real-life couple sexuality. Maura began to question her assumption that Dan needed a spontaneous erection to reassure her that she was loved. A problem with the Best Friend sexual style is the demand that all sex be loving, mutual, functional, and serve to assure the partner that everything is fine. Maura became aware of her discomfort with playful and especially erotic scenarios. Valuing intercourse was great, but it was for the wrong reasons. Intercourse was a test of love and attraction rather than part of the pleasuring/eroticism couple process.

Dan wanted Maura and he to be intimate and erotic friends who valued sexuality while recognizing that couple sexuality has many possible roles, meanings, and outcomes. Dan was convinced that the Complementary sexual style was the right fit for him and their marriage. This would give them the freedom and flexibility to be open to a range of scenarios and techniques which included intercourse, but was not limited to intercourse. The Complementary sexual style encourages touching and sexuality. Dan felt the Best Friend sexual style was too demanding and smothered sexual play and creativity. Instead of fostering mutuality and playfulness it was the "tyranny of mutuality" and the "demand for perfect intercourse". Dan was enthusiastic about the Complementary couple sexual style because it emphasized personal responsibility for sex and being an intimate sexual team; because both he and Maura valued intimacy and eroticism; because she had her bridges to desire, he had his bridges to desire, and they had their bridges to desire; because both synchronous and asynchronous sexual encounters were accepted; and because it embraced Good Enough Sex (GES) rather than demanding perfect individual sex performance. He believed (Maura found this difficult to accept) that couple sexuality could have a range of roles, meanings, and outcomes.

Maura accepted most of Dan's ideas and felt good about his sexual enthusiasm for her and their marriage. She agreed the Complementary sexual style would be a better fit than her idealistic Best Friend sexual style. She realized that some elements of the Complementary sexual style would be a challenge for her. Much of her intercourse focus came from the belief that this is what "should" happen rather than her genuine preferences. In addition, she was not comfortable with nudity and non-demand pleasuring. Clothes coming off quickly and starting intercourse as soon as possible was not so much a preference as a way to avoid self-consciousness. Before becoming a couple, Maura's experience with men and "foreplay" had been awkward—she'd felt self-conscious and pressured. She preferred intercourse to foreplay. She was not comfortable with giving or receiving touching, especially genital stimulation. This was a new insight for Dan, who had not understood why Maura could enjoy affection and kissing, but not sensual, playful, or erotic touch. He had felt ignored by her sexually (other than intercourse), but now had greater awareness and empathy. He wanted to be her sexual ally, not coerce or intimidate her.

Dan was surprised when Maura said that she would be more comfortable if they began with her giving manual penile stimulation while being receptive to Dan's manual, kissing, sensual, and playful stimulation.

This reduced her self-consciousness and opened new experiences of pleasure. Dan suggested taking turns with giving and receiving, but Maura preferred mutual touching.

For Maura, a key component of the Complementary sexual style was the understanding that Dan enjoyed pleasuring her. Maura admitted that although she enjoyed intercourse and was orgasmic during intercourse, some of the time she faked orgasm. With their new couple sexual style, Maura delayed transitioning to intercourse until she was into an erotic flow rather than rushing to intercourse. Maura discovered that if she allowed herself one or two "small orgasms" before intromission, it was easier to be orgasmic during intercourse. She felt more sexually open and responsive when stimulation was mutual. This was fine with Dan since he preferred mutual and multiple stimulation. Maura embraced their Complementary couple sexual style. Dan didn't need Maura to be a sexual clone. He appreciated her acceptance of giving and receiving stimulation before and during intercourse. What they valued about being a Complementary sexual couple was awareness of the multiple roles, meanings, and outcomes of couple sexuality.

## Exercise: Choosing the Right Couple Sexual Style for You

This exercise asks you to discuss the concept of couple sexual styles and decide the right sexual style for you and your relationship. Be aware of the guidelines about relational and sexual styles. Make a decision based on what is the right fit for you. Remember, this is a couple decision.

Read about the four couple sexual styles. Each partner has the power to veto at least one and up to two sexual styles. This leaves two to three styles which are a possibility for you. Next, choose the style that each partner feels is the best fit. Ideally, you choose the same sexual style. If you have chosen different sexual styles, discuss the attitudes, behaviors, emotions, and values which attract you to that style. Remember, a healthy relationship is based on a positive influence process, do not pressure or coerce your partner. The decision about a sexual style is at its core a couple process. What is the sexual style that is the best fit for your relationship? We advocate for the Complementary couple sexual style, but not for all couples. Be sure your decision is positively motivated and fits you and your relationship.

A specific suggestion when it is difficult to decide is for you to play out a couple sexual style for one month and then a second couple sexual style the next month. This gives you a real-life experience of implementing two different styles to see which is the best fit for you attitudinally, behaviorally, and emotionally. Remember the core guideline: sexuality has a 15–20% role of energizing your bond and reinforcing feelings of desire and desirability. Your chosen couple sexual style determines the way you balance personal autonomy with being an intimate sexual team and how you integrate intimacy and eroticism.

Be clear and specific about what you value as regards your chosen couple sexual style. Even more importantly, be specific about how to implement your sexual style so that it promotes desire/pleasure/eroticism/satisfaction. Both partners value your chosen couple sexual style.

Each couple sexual style has its own set of potential vulnerabilities. Luckily, you don't need to be aware of all potential vulnerabilities. Be clear about the one to three vulnerabilities which could impact your couple sexual style. Write them down so that each partner is aware. For example, a major vulnerability of the Complementary couple sexual style is taking it for granted and allowing sexuality to become mediocre. A second vulnerability is that as your life and relationship change (birth of a child, an illness or disability, change in financial status) you ignore its impact on couple sexuality.

The next step is to develop a specific plan to challenge the vulnerability of your chosen sexual style so that couple sexuality remains vital and satisfying. Awareness is important, but more important is putting time and energy into maintaining strong, resilient sexual desire.

Another suggestion is to check-in as a couple at least once a year to ensure that your sexual style continues to be the right fit. Discuss feelings and requests to enhance couple sexual vitality and satisfaction. Most couples affirm their relational and sexual styles. However, you can make changes to ensure sexuality remains a positive part of your lives and relationship, whether you've been a couple for five or 35 years. For example, for the Traditional couple sexual style, the man initiates an intimacy/pleasuring date with a prohibition on intercourse every six months. The woman initiates a playful or erotic date once every six months and she decides whether it will transition to intercourse or not. Value your chosen couple sexual style while adding "spice" so that sex roles are not rigid.

## Summary

An empowering insight is that your relational and sexual styles are usually different. Engage in dialogue about the sexual style which is the best fit for you and promotes desire/pleasure/eroticism/satisfaction. This allows both of you to be your authentic sexual self while remaining an intimate sexual team.

The most common decision is to choose the Best Friend relational style and the Complementary sexual style. Ensure that your couple sexual style remains vital and satisfying so that sexuality has a 15–20% role for you personally and relationally.

## 9

## PERSONAL RESPONSIBILITY / INTIMATE SEXUAL TEAM

You are responsible for your sexual desire and orgasm. Own your "sexual voice" (autonomy). It is not your partner's responsibility to make you desirous or orgasmic. Yet, at its core sexuality is an intimate team process. The challenge is to integrate your sexual voice with being an intimate sexual team.

This one—two approach of personal responsibility/intimate team is key to healthy sexuality. This is the opposite of the movie/love song/"pop sex" cultural messages that the sexual key is being unconditionally loved and erotically turned-on by your partner. You never see marital sex in the movies, it is always a new couple (dating or an affair). Both partners are turned-on before any touching. Sex is fast, dramatic, erotic, perfect, with both partners easily orgasmic or multi-orgasmic. We tell couples that if you have "Hollywood" type sex once a month you are better than 95% of couples. The destructive media message is that you are "not good enough sexually". Positive, realistic sexual expectations are crucial for satisfying couple sexuality.

Couples value sexual experiences which are mutual and synchronous. This means that both partners experience desire/pleasure/eroticism/satisfaction. The best couple sexuality is mutual and synchronous. However, even among happily married, sexually functional couples most experiences are asynchronous. This means the sex was better for one partner than the other. Asynchronous couple sexuality is not only normal, it is healthy. You are not sexual clones. You have your own sexual preferences and feelings—you are a unique sexual person. Asynchronous sexuality is embraced as long as it's not at the expense of the partner or relationship (Girard & Woolley, 2017). Expressing your unique, authentic sexual self is good for your relationship.

Positive, realistic sexual expectations based on the Good Enough Sex (GES) model affirms couple sexuality. This includes that it is normal for 5–15% of sexual encounters to be dissatisfying or dysfunctional. Whether once a month or once a year, it is normal to have lousy sex. The media hides this fact from the public, but a crucial understanding is that sexuality has a range of roles, meanings, and outcomes (Gillespie, 2017). When you have a negative experience, accept this without guilt or blaming. Acceptance is key to healthy sexuality. Another key is to turn toward your partner, not pretend or avoid. Your partner is your intimate and erotic friend whether the sexual experience was wonderful, okay, or dysfunctional. Acceptance is especially important when dealing with sexual dysfunction. When you accept your partner, it is easier to address and resolve the sexual problem as an intimate team.

## Personal Responsibility for Sexuality

You are a sexual person from the day you are born until the day you die. The key for personal responsibility is to understand and accept your "authentic sexual self". Unless you accept yourself, you cannot expect your partner to accept you. This is true whether your authentic sexual self involves traditional sexual values or your sexual self is gay or "kinky". Acceptance of your authentic sexual self involves all your attitudes, behaviors, and feelings including sad, painful, or traumatic experiences (Meston, Rellini & Heiman, 2006). This asks a lot of you. So many people have a "contingent sexual self-esteem", believing if their partner knew everything about them sexually they would not respect or love them. That's a very hard way to live. This would cause you to feel like a "sexual fraud" and fear discovery.

Accepting your authentic sexual self does not mean going on a talk show and sharing everything with a radio, TV, or internet audience. It means being personally aware and owning all your positive and negative sexual experiences.

The most destructive of human emotions is shame. Shame is very different than feeling bad or guilty about a sexual experience. Shame involves feeling controlled by a negative experience and allowing it to define you as a person. Feeling regret or guilt about past sexual behavior can motivate change. Shame keeps you stuck in self-defeating sexual patterns. The more shameful you feel the more likely you will continue self-destructive sexuality. Rather than being responsible for your sexuality, shame controls your sexual behavior and self-esteem.

A crucial concept is you can learn from the past, but you cannot change the past. Your power for sexual change is in the present and future (McCarthy, 2015). When you own your sexual story, you accept both positive and negative experiences—including all your sexual attitudes, behaviors, and feelings. People fall into the traps of either denying negative sexual experiences or giving them inordinate power. Examples include an unwanted pregnancy, sexual abuse in childhood or adolescence, contracting a sexually transmitted infection, being sexually harassed or humiliated, shame about masturbation, feeling embarrassed about sexual fantasies, and being shocked at learning something sexual about their parents or other family members. In a perfect world these would not occur. However, by age 25 a substantial majority of both women and men have had at least one negative sexual experience (most people have two or more) (Rellini, 2014). The challenge is to accept and learn from these experiences, but not allow them to control your sexual self-esteem. For example, most young men begin their sexual lives as premature ejaculators. With increased practice and comfort, the majority learn ejaculatory control (intercourse which lasts 3–9 minutes and you feel in control of when you ejaculate). Rather than being embarrassed by the past, accept and enjoy intercourse with good (not perfect) ejaculatory control. A female example is the young woman who had strong fears of an unwanted pregnancy and found intercourse anxiety provoking. Sex was both exciting and worrisome. When you obtain an IUD, you can feel good about yourself using a long-acting reversible form of contraception (LARC) and embrace the reliability of effective contraception. You are an aware, responsible woman who protects her sexual health.

Rather than feeling embarrassed or guilty about the past, accept past sexual experiences and take pride in being a healthy sexual person in the present. Discovering your authentic sexual self involves a range of feelings and experiences, including confusion and missteps. These are best understood as part of your learning process. Even the most regretted sexual experiences contain important learnings, if only who you are not. Regret those sexual experiences, but do not be ashamed of them. Examples include obtaining an abortion, contracting Chlamydia, or being in a destructive relationship which dragged on for over a year. Don't let those experiences define you. Personal responsibility for sexuality means a positive view of yourself as a sexual person with sexuality having an integral 15–20% role in your life and relationship. Acceptance is the foundation, followed by making wise sexual decisions in the present and future.

A particularly challenging issue for personal responsibility is how you deal with intimacy and eroticism. Typically, these dimensions have been split by gender—women valuing intimacy and men valuing eroticism. Our recommended strategy is integrative—both the woman and man value intimacy and eroticism. We advise against splitting sexual dimensions. In the desire/pleasure/eroticism/satisfaction mantra both intimacy and eroticism are integral to female, male, and couple sexuality. These are very different dimensions. Intimacy involves warm, loving, predictable, secure, and sensual feelings and touch. Eroticism involves mystery, creativity, unpredictability, socially unacceptable fantasies, dramatic sensations and feelings. Although different, intimacy and eroticism are not adversarial or incompatible. Ideally both partners value intimacy and eroticism. The trap for women is to view eroticism as the man's domain and lose her sexual voice, especially her erotic voice. The trap for men is to de-eroticize the partner and undervalue sexual intimacy and pleasurable touch. Integrated eroticism is healthy for the woman, man, and couple. Rather than feeling intimidated by the porn approach or the illicit, dramatic model of eroticism, develop erotic scenarios and techniques which facilitate vital, satisfying sexuality. This usually involves partner interaction arousal/eroticism. You being turned-on facilitates your partner's arousal and establishes a positive feedback cycle. The major aphrodisiac is an involved, aroused partner. Rather than sexual games or visual turn-ons, partner interaction arousal/eroticism features mutual turn-ons. Of course, a negative sexual feedback cycle can occur—you feeling sexually turned-off is a turn-off for your partner. Sometimes turn-offs are manipulative or exploitive. However, most couples benefit from the positive feedback cycle of partner interaction arousal. Partner interaction arousal does not require mutual, synchronous sexual response, but does benefit from partner receptivity and responsivity.

The second most common arousal/eroticism pattern is self-entrancement arousal. This involves one partner giving pleasure and the other receiving. A core factor in self-entrancement arousal is that the receiving partner is mindful, not passive. Provide the type of touching you enjoy giving rather than focusing on "turning on" your partner in the traditional "foreplay" scenario. Use of self-entrancement arousal increases with aging. In terms of personal responsibility, the active partner enjoys giving pleasure. Your pleasure is enhanced by the receiving partner's sexual responsivity. The receiving partner is open to pleasurable sensations and feelings. Allow yourself to go with the pleasurable/erotic feelings and sensations.

The third arousal/eroticism style is role enactment arousal. This is the eroticism/arousal style featured on internet sites and advocated in the sexual media, but is the least used. Role enactment arousal/eroticism involves using external resources including sexual toys, watching X-rated videos, using blindfolds or handcuffs, "rough" sex, being sexual outdoors or in front of a mirror, acting out an erotic fantasy. In role enactment arousal the external stimuli provide a powerful erotic charge. Role enactment arousal focuses on eroticism, and downplays intimacy and pleasuring. Traditionally, role enactment arousal focuses on the man's sexual preferences. Each partner has their erotic voice and preferred scenarios and techniques.

## Fantasies vs. Behavior

A core issue is the role and meaning of erotic fantasies. Most men and women utilize erotic fantasies, especially for masturbation. In addition, a majority of men and a significant number of women utilize erotic fantasy during couple sex, on occasion if not regularly.

The contentious issue is how to understand the role of sexual fantasy. Is fantasy like an x-ray, revealing your genuine sexual desire? Scientifically, the data demonstrate that for the overwhelming majority of people fantasy and real-life sexual behavior are two very different realms (Renaud & Byers, 2001). What gives fantasies an erotic charge is they are totally different than real-life couple sexuality. Typically, if you play out an erotic fantasy the result will be a sexual "dud". What is erotically inviting in fantasy turns out to be awkward and disappointing, raising self-consciousness. There is nothing as anti-erotic as self-consciousness.

Couples accept the role of erotic fantasy as a bridge to desire or a bridge to erotic flow and orgasm. By their nature erotic fantasies are not socially acceptable. Almost no one fantasizes about being sexual with your spouse in the bedroom in the missionary position. You fantasize about being sexual with an inappropriate partner, being forced or sexually forcing a partner, observing or being observed sexually, a group sex or orgy scenario, or being sexual with someone of the same gender. Is that what you really want? No, but it serves as a highly charged erotic fantasy.

What causes major problems is the combination of secrecy, eroticism, and shame. It is like taking a "poison pill". Sex becomes highly secretive, narrow, compulsive, and controlling. Women and men use erotic fantasy to enhance sexuality. However, when you combine secrecy, eroticism, and shame this takes over your sexuality.

Authentic sexual self-esteem incorporates your attitudes, experiences, emotions, and values. This includes the right to your private erotic fantasies. Don't allow fantasy to control your sexuality.

Can or should you share erotic fantasies with your partner? "Pop sex" internet sites and popular books urge you to disclose and play out fantasies to enhance your sexual life. Although it is important to respect individual differences realizing that "sexually, one size never fits all", for most couples sharing fantasies is self-defeating advice. Fantasy and behavior are two very different domains. You have a right to your private erotic fantasies. Sharing fantasies, especially the details, is usually unwise and sometimes has negative consequences for one or both partners. "Pop sex" advice about sexual freedom can result in anti-erotic experiences. The first step is personal responsibility for sexuality. Now let's consider the second step—being a sexual team.

## Intimate Sexual Team

Sexuality is a team sport. Being a sexual team does not mean giving up your sexual autonomy, it means integrating your sexual self into your relationship. Most couples have traditional values, which involves prioritizing your intimate sexual relationship. Share desire/pleasure/eroticism/satisfaction with your life partner (spouse). This includes being both intimate and erotic friends. Integration of intimacy and eroticism is a major couple challenge.

In Chapter 8, we discussed the importance of developing a couple sexual style. Your sexual style is usually different from your relational style. Be sure your couple sexual style is acceptable to both partners and facilitates desire/pleasure/eroticism/satisfaction. Whether your sexual style is Complementary, Traditional, Best Friend, or Emotionally Expressive, the crucial factor is sexuality as a positive resource in your relationship.

We advocate the Complementary couple sexual style for most (not all) couples. The Complementary sexual style is the best fit because it follows the model of personal responsibility and being an intimate sexual team. You promote female—male sexual equity with both partners valuing intimacy and eroticism. In addition, you have her, his, and their bridges to sexual desire. Your sexual style recognizes the multiple roles, meanings, and outcomes of couple sexuality. The Complementary style affirms both synchronous and asynchronous sexual experiences to be dissatisfying or dysfunctional. It supports Good Enough Sex (GES), including that it is normal for 5–15% of sexual experiences to be mediocre, dissatisfying, or dysfunctional.

The other couple sexual styles—Traditional, Best Friend, Emotionally Expressive—can be healthy. Be sure your sexual style is the right fit for your feelings and values. Enjoy the strengths of your chosen couple sexual style. Also, be aware of potential traps so you do not fall into these.

A strength of the Traditional sexual style is clear gender expectations—eroticism and intercourse are the man's domain, and intimacy and relational stability are the woman's domain. The potential traps are that the roles become rigid and resentment builds. The strengths of the Best Friend sexual style are the emphasis on intimacy and security. The traps are de-eroticizing the partner and the overemphasis on mutuality causing low sexual frequency. The strengths of the Emotionally Expressive sexual style are the vibrancy of erotic scenarios and taking sexual risks. The traps are breaking boundaries and emotionally wearing out each other and draining your relationship.

Being an intimate sexual team reinforces the desire/pleasure/eroticism/satisfaction mantra. You turn toward each other as intimate and erotic allies whether the sexual experience was wonderful or dysfunctional. You trust that sexually "my partner has my back".

## May and Eric

May and Eric are both 29 years old and have been a couple for three years (married 19 months). Only recently have they created a balance of being responsible for self sexually and being an intimate sexual team. In retrospect, they realize sex issues almost subverted their relationship both before marriage and in the first year of the marriage.

May and Eric met at an alumni happy hour (they had attended a large state university) in the city they now live and work in. Although in the same academic year, May did not remember meeting Eric. Eric knew one of her friends, but only had a vague remembrance of May. At the happy hour, they shared interests and discovered a mutual attraction. Their early relationship experiences were filled with intrigue and promise. May enjoyed Eric's enthusiasm for travel and spontaneous adventures. May was interested in an intimate relationship, but Eric was hesitant. He had grown cynical about romantic/sexual relationships and fallen into the pattern of hook-up sex. His preference was women who were tall and very slim, quite different than 5' 2" May who weighed 120 pounds. May realized she could not become taller for Eric. She has a positive body image and Eric would either accept her for who she was or not. This is a core concept for individual self-esteem. May needed to accept herself sexually and feel desire and desirability as she was.

Eric split sexual and emotional factors. Eric thought of himself as a pro-sexual man and a good person who did not harass or abuse women. However, he split intimacy and eroticism. This was clear to May, but not to Eric. May felt Eric was a good boyfriend and she enjoyed their sexual relationship, but felt that he didn't value her as part of an intimate sexual team. May and Eric were a sexually functional couple, but sexuality was not special or energizing. May was aware of the difference between functional sex and intimate, satisfying couple sexuality, but this was a concept Eric had not considered.

As the relationship progressed, May became more attached to Eric, but did not feel they were growing as an intimate sexual team. When May raised the idea of entering couple therapy with a clinician who specialized in intimacy and sexuality issues, Eric was taken aback. Like several of his college-educated peers, Eric had been in short-term therapy focused on adjustment issues, but had not dealt with intimacy or sexuality issues. He viewed therapy as more for the woman than the man and felt defensive about May's request for couple therapy. Yet, he realized there was something missing in their relationship. Like so many men of his generation, Eric had low expectations of sexuality in an intimate relationship. He enjoyed May and their sexual relationship but saw intimacy and relational stability as the woman's domain, not a shared domain. Eric's sexual experiences had been positive for a few months to a year and then lost their specialness. His naïve assumption was he would know when the perfect woman came along and everything, including intimacy and sexuality, would naturally flow. Eric did not take personal responsibility for sexuality. With great ambivalence, Eric agreed to see a couple therapist. He was pleased that May suggested a male therapist, so Eric would not feel ganged up on.

The therapist began with a couple session to reinforce that intimacy and sexuality are best understood as a couple issue. Sessions two and three were individual psychological/relational/sexual histories which allowed the clinician to understand May and Eric's personal strengths and vulnerabilities. The fourth session involved the therapist giving each spouse feedback while the partner listened. Typically, at least 30% (often more) of the material is new to the partner. Creating a genuine individual narrative is the foundation for a therapy plan. This session bridges the assessment and treatment phases.

May and Eric agreed to a six-month good faith effort to create a new couple sexual style focused on desire and satisfaction. The challenge for May was to affirm the integrity of her sexual voice (sexual self-esteem) while creating a couple sexuality where she felt desire and genuinely desired. The challenge for Eric was to increase intimacy and sexual involvement. Eric needed to assume responsibility for himself emotionally and sexually, not look to May to prove herself to him. This feedback was an "aha" moment for May. It was not her role to prove her sexual worth to Eric. It was Eric's responsibility to learn to enhance and value couple sexuality. Eric had to meet his challenges rather than depend on May to do it for him.

Eric needed to "show-up" for the challenge of integrating intimacy and eroticism into their relationship. For Eric, eroticism had been tied to fantasy and illicit sex, not integrated eroticism. This challenge was an example of the personal responsibility/intimate sexual team model. May could be his ally, but was not responsible for changing him.

Eric learned to better utilize partner interaction arousal/eroticism and self-entrancement arousal/eroticism. For partner interaction arousal Eric embraced May's arousal to touching and erotic scenarios so her arousal enhanced his arousal. Eric's old pattern was to overutilize fantasies of young, slim women who "serviced" him sexually. Effective use of erotic fantasy involves a bridge to arousal during partner sex. Eric had misused fantasy as a wall to block May out. May enjoyed erotic fantasies, they enhanced her erotic response. Her fantasies were a special erotic charge which enhanced sexual feelings, especially touching and being touched. She wasn't dependent on erotic fantasies; instead she used them to facilitate being sexually present with Eric. Rather than blocking her out, Eric let May in to share intimacy, pleasure, and eroticism. He felt present sexually in a new, genuine manner. Eric's sexual response enhanced May's sexual response. Eric learned that the sexual key was to value touch stimuli, not be dependent on visual stimuli. Previously, Eric had kept his eyes closed in order to focus on erotic fantasies. This provided an "aha" moment for Eric. Fantasy could have the function of being a bridge to couple eroticism, not used as a wall to distance him from May.

The focus was different for self-entrancement arousal/eroticism. Eric's system of foreplay had been to arouse May so she was ready for intercourse. He was the active, in charge partner, aroused by her passivity. In his erotic fantasies, Eric was turned-on by women (never May) being out of control and lustful, driven to deep throat fellatio.

May was open to self-entrancement arousal, but wanted a very different scenario. May didn't want to be "worked on", but to be mindful and sexually open. She wanted to give pleasure and eroticism rather than "service" Eric. They had a frank dialogue about Eric's approach to "blow jobs" which May found off-putting. She enjoyed taking turns giving and receiving oral stimulation (an example of self-entrancement arousal), but hated feeling she was an actress in Eric's porn video. The challenge for Eric was to receive oral sex from his intimate partner rather than viewing this as an erotic performance.

This dialogue crystalized what it meant to be responsible for yourself sexually and be an intimate sexual team. You must be a healthy sexual person to be an intimate sexual team.

## Exercise: Personal Responsibility/Intimate Sexual Team

This is a two-phase exercise. First, be honest with yourself and disclose to your partner your authentic sexual self. This requires you to disclose attitudes, feelings, values, and sexual experiences—recognizing and sharing both strengths and vulnerabilities. Be accepting of who you are sexually. How do you feel about intimacy? How do you feel about pleasure? How do you feel about eroticism? Give genuine responses, not socially desirable answers. What allows you to feel good about yourself as a sexual person? What do you want to add or try out to make your sexual experience more satisfying? You have a right to sexual autonomy (privacy), especially your erotic fantasies. However, you don't have the right to hide behind sexual embarrassment or guilt. Own your sexual voice and share it with your partner. Sexuality can have a healthy, integral role in your life. Share one to three things that you previously had not incorporated into your authentic sexual self and dialogue with your partner about sexual self-acceptance.

The second phase of this exercise is even more challenging and important. What do you need in order to be an intimate sexual team? This is so much more than intercourse frequency. As a team, do you genuinely value desire/pleasure/eroticism/satisfaction? Do you share both intimacy and eroticism?

Ultimately, sex is a team sport, not an individual performance. What is the right sexual style for you, so desire remains strong and resilient? Have a clear, specific dialogue about what is the best balance of autonomy and being a sexual team. Next, dialogue about how to integrate intimacy and eroticism in your relationship. For most couples we advocate adopting the Complementary couple sexual style. However, that is not the right fit for all couples. Jointly affirm the sexual style which is the right fit for you.

The next step is to implement your chosen couple sexual style. Insights and good intentions are not enough. Ensure that your couple sexual style genuinely promotes desire/pleasure/eroticism/satisfaction. Develop a sexual initiation system so there is a regular rhythm of sexual connection. Is sexuality, especially pleasure-oriented touching, free of pressure and coercion? Do each of you feel comfortable giving and receiving pleasure? How do you transition to erotic scenarios and techniques? Do you prefer partner interaction arousal, self-entrancement arousal, or role enactment arousal? Identify erotic scenarios or techniques which are a turn-off. Do you have the freedom to veto those? How and when do you transition to intercourse? Does intercourse feel like a natural transition from the pleasuring/eroticism process or is it an individual pass–fail performance? Do you enjoy multiple stimulation during intercourse? What is your preferred orgasmic pattern? Do you enjoy afterplay? What are your favorite afterplay scenarios?

Be honest as you dialogue about being a sexual couple. What are the cultural stereotypes you need to explore and challenge? What do you want to add to your couple sexual repertoire? What do you want to drop from your couple sexual repertoire? Dialogue is important, but it's not enough. It is crucial to implement healthy attitudes, feelings, values, and experiences into couple sexuality. This exercise asks you to integrate personal responsibility for sexuality with being an intimate sexual team.

## Summary

The concept of balance is important in all areas of health, including sexual health. A crucial balance is being personally responsible for sexuality while being an intimate sexual team. Unless you have the right to your authentic sexual self, you cannot feel part of an intimate sexual team. Be self-accepting and feel accepted by your partner. Acceptance provides the foundation for change and is the basis for a positive influence process.

The essence of healthy sexuality is giving and receiving pleasure-oriented touch. The challenge is to develop a mutually agreed on couple sexual style which integrates intimacy and eroticism. As an intimate sexual team, enhance desire/pleasure/eroticism/satisfaction. Turn toward your partner whether the sex was great, good, mediocre, or dysfunctional. Accept that couple sexuality can have a range of roles, meanings, and outcomes. This promotes sexual desire and satisfaction.

# 10

# THE PARADOX OF SEXUALITY

Is sex the major factor in life for you and your relationship? No. In fact, the role of sexuality is paradoxical. Healthy sexuality has a small (15–20%) yet integral role. Sexuality energizes your couple bond and reinforces feelings of desire and desirability. Your challenge is to create genuine sexual self-esteem. You are a proud sexual person and can express your sexuality so that it honors your authentic sexual self. The paradox is that dysfunctional, conflictual, or avoidant sexuality has a powerful destabilizing role. Sexuality is the enemy, not the friend. Rather than the 15–20% role, sex causes hurt, anger, depression, or alienation. Rather than a shared pleasure, sex is a source of demands, conflicts, threats, and a weapon against your partner (McCarthy & Ross, 2017).

The paradox is that unhealthy sexuality has a more powerful negative role than the role of healthy sexuality. Sex cannot save a relationship, but sex can destroy a relationship. Reinforce the healthy roles and meanings of sexuality for you and your relationship so that it continues to be a positive factor throughout your life. You cannot take sex for granted nor treat it with benign neglect. Confront unhealthy sexuality so that it does not subvert your life and relationship. You deserve to give and receive pleasure-oriented touch. Reinforcing healthy sexuality is not enough. You need to confront unhealthy sexual attitudes, behaviors, values, and emotions. There are a range of negative sexuality sources in our culture. Healthy sexuality and unhealthy sexuality are two separate dimensions. You need to attend to both.

## Healthy Individual and Couple Sexuality

Healthy sexuality affirms that sex is a good thing in life, not bad. Sexuality is integral to you as a woman or man. The question, whether you are 18, 48, or 78; straight or gay; single, married, divorced, or partnered; is whether sexuality has a positive or negative role in your life. If sexuality is not having a positive role, you can change attitudes, behaviors, and feelings to make it positive. You deserve healthy sexuality as an individual and couple.

A key is to accept your "authentic sexual self" whether you are a traditional person in a traditional relationship or have non-traditional sexual values and are in a non-traditional relationship. Traditional is not just heterosexual marriage. Traditional means you prioritize your relationship and have an emotional and sexual commitment to monogamy. Partnered, lesbian, and a significant number of gay couples are traditional. Chapters 13 and 14 explore non-traditional sexual behavior and values. The most common issue is consensual non-monogamy. In addition, non-traditional individuals might value sexual friendships, polyamory, or pansexuality. Non-traditional individuals and couples deserve sexuality to have a positive role in their lives.

Sex is not the major factor in life. Sex should not control your self-esteem or relationship. Sexuality is healthiest when it has an integral, positive function. Being a pro-sexual person adds vitality and satisfaction to your life. Sex energizes you and helps you make "wise" personal and relationship decisions.

Psychological well-being is promoted when your attitudes, behaviors, and feelings are congruent, including sexually. Own your "sexual voice" (autonomy), which includes your "erotic voice" and "orgasmic voice". Rather than worrying you are not perfect sexually, accept who you are with your strengths and vulnerabilities. Many people have a "contingent sexual self-esteem". You don't accept your sexual self or history. You treat your sexual past as a "shameful secret". Contingent self-esteem is a hard way to live. Healthy sexuality includes accepting the sad and vulnerable parts of yourself. Honor these sexual learnings, but don't give them control of your sexual self-esteem.

The essence of sexual self-esteem is acceptance and feeling that you deserve pleasure. It is not contingent on everything being perfect. Accept yourself with the positives and negatives from your sexual past. Even more importantly, accept yourself in the present with your psychological, relational, and sexual strengths and vulnerabilities. Being "pro-sexual" involves self-acceptance so sexuality has a positive role in your life and relationship.

## The 15–20% Role of Sexuality

A healthy marriage/relationship involves a respectful, trusting, emotional commitment. People value a traditional relationship where the couple bond is prioritized with a commitment to monogamy. Sex is not, nor should it be, the most important factor in your relationship. Sexuality has a 15–20% role of energizing your bond and reinforcing feelings of desire and desirability. In our culture, the overemphasis on a loving, magical sexual relationship which overcomes any personal or relational problem is self-defeating. We are pro-sexual, but are not proponents of magical or perfectionistic sex. This makes for great movies and novels, but not for real-life couples. Healthy couple sexuality has a variety of roles, meanings, and outcomes. Sometimes sex can be dramatic and magical, but most often it is a shared pleasure, to reinforce intimacy (especially after or before a sexual encounter), and sex as a tension reducer to help you cope with the stresses of life and a relationship. Couple sexuality is variable and flexible with multiple roles and outcomes. The 15–20% role includes enhancing attachment, sharing touch, a means to reconnect after disappointment or conflict, feeling silly and playful, sharing warmth and intimacy, orgasm for tension reduction, celebrating a job promotion, or spicing up a boring day.

Healthy sexuality is a combination of individual autonomy and being an intimate sexual team. Value your sexual self, your partner's sexuality, and being a sexual couple.

## Couple Dimensions of Healthy Sexuality

At its core sexuality is a team process of sharing pleasure. The challenge is to integrate intimacy and eroticism in your relationship. Discovering your couple sexual style is a joint task. The best sex is mutual and synchronous. Be aware that often the sexual encounter has a different meaning and outcome for each partner. Accept sexuality which is sometimes wonderful and special, other times excellent for one partner and good for the other, at times asynchronous (meeting one partner's needs while the other is "going along for the ride"), sometimes mediocre or unsatisfying, and other times dysfunctional. Whether dissatisfying or dysfunctional sex occurs 5 or 15% of the time, the challenge is to turn toward each other as intimate friends who do not blame or make one another feel guilty. Healthy sexuality is anti-perfectionistic. You are there for each other whether sex is great, good, okay, mediocre, or dysfunctional. The key is to turn toward your partner, with no blame and no apology.

Recognize that the sexual encounter can have different motivations and outcomes. For one partner sex can be a symbol of loving feelings while for the other it is a tension reducer to deal with fall-out from a parenting problem. Another time, sex can be for one partner a way to reconnect after time apart, while for the other it is driven by the need for orgasm. Sometimes you want a hug, other times an orgasm. Sexuality can be a means of sharing sadness for one partner while an anxiety reducer for the other. It is not unusual for the role and meaning of sex to change in the middle of the encounter. For example, one partner might begin in an uninvolved manner, but as the scenario plays out, she becomes highly aroused. In another example, one partner might begin desirous, but become distracted and choose to switch to a sensual scenario.

Believing that every sexual encounter must be mutual, intimate, erotic, with intercourse and orgasm is an unrealistic demand which leads to frustration and low desire. Couples who accept and embrace variable, flexible Good Enough Sex (GES) have a vital relational resource. This is not the sex of novels and movies, rather it is the sexuality of loving and satisfied couples. GES is much superior to the perfect individual sex performance model.

For most couples, the Complementary couple sexual style is the best fit. It allows each partner to have their "sexual voice" while being securely bonded. In the Complementary sexual style, each partner affirms the value of intimacy and eroticism. Each can initiate and have the power of veto—to say "no" to a sexual scenario or technique. Both partners accept both synchronous and asynchronous sexuality, recognizing that healthy couple sexuality affirms a range of roles, meanings, and outcomes.

The vulnerabilities and challenges are different for other couple sexual styles. The vulnerabilities for the Traditional sexual style are that the roles become too rigid and the woman resents that the man's demand for intercourse overrides her desire for intimacy and flexible couple sexuality. The vulnerabilities for the Best Friend sexual style are there is such an emphasis on intimacy and mutuality that the partners do not make sexual initiations or take risks, so frequency is low and they de-eroticize the partner and relationship. The vulnerabilities for the Emotionally Expressive sexual style are that the need for variety and erotic intensity becomes a drain and disrupts the relationship. Being aware of the vulnerabilities and working together to meet those challenges allows sexuality to maintain a healthy role in your life and relationship.

Establishing couple sexuality is the easier task. The challenge is to maintain sexual desire and satisfaction. You cannot take sexuality for granted nor can sexuality rest on its laurels. You need thought, intentionality, communication, and energy to maintain a vital sexual relationship. A key is unpredictable sexual scenarios and techniques. The enemy of sexual desire is routine, predictable sex which always leads to intercourse. Although we strongly advocate for intercourse and orgasm, totally predictable sex subverts desire. Mixing sensual, playful, erotic, and intercourse touch facilitates strong, resilient desire. By its nature couple sexuality is variable and flexible. The best sex is mutual and synchronous. However, demanding that all sex be mutual and synchronous undercuts desire and satisfaction. There is not one right way to be a sexual couple. Healthy couple sexuality is based on positive, realistic expectations adopted from the GES model.

## Confronting the Negative Role of Individual Sexuality

Both women and men can be secretive or shameful about sexuality. They have a contingent sexual self-esteem, believing that if their partner or others knew their sexual history they would not be accepted or loved. This is a hard way to live, and dominates their sexuality. Rather than sex having a positive role, it has a powerful negative role. This not only subverts sexuality, it negates their self-esteem, relationship, and life.

The sexual experiences which cause the greatest problems are child sexual abuse, rape, and incest. The best estimate is that by age 25 approximately 40% of women and one in six men have experienced the "big three" (Boney-McCoy & Finkelhor, 1995). Even more striking is that by age 25 over 90% of both women and men have had a negative, confusing, or guilt-inducing sexual experience. This includes an unwanted pregnancy, contracting an STI, being exhibited to, being sexually harassed or humiliated, caught masturbating, shame about sexual fantasies, sexual rejection or dysfunction, feeling guilty about a sexual experience. This data is not to minimize sexual trauma, but to destigmatize these experiences and realize that you are not alone. Negative sexual experiences are almost universal and need not be a source of shame. More than the sexual incident itself, letting it be a shameful secret gives it more power than it deserves. A contingent self-esteem dominates your life. Even when the person's adult sexual life is fine, there is fear about their past or fear that something bad will happen in the present which will trigger guilt, anger, fear, or shame about their sexual past.

Negative sexual incidents can happen in the present. Denying them or feeling shameful takes over your sexual self-esteem. Bad sexual experiences happen to good people. More than the experience itself, how you deal with it is the important factor. Accepting negative sexual experiences and learning from them allows sexuality to maintain its healthy role. Making it a shameful secret results in giving this experience control so that sexuality becomes the enemy that controls you.

## Confronting the Destructive Role of Couple Sexuality

Sexual problems are the major cause of relational break-up in the first five years of marriage (or a partnered relationship). Sexual difficulties are the most common mental health problem in culture; more common than anxiety and depression combined. Sadly, sexual problems are not addressed in therapy (Binik & Hall, 2014).

The traditional model had been to consider a sexual problem as a symptom of a relationship problem with the mistaken belief that when the relationship improves the sex problem will automatically be resolved. Sexual problems, especially desire problems, must be directly addressed to promote change. In the past 20 years the medical community and the culture (promoted by a vigorous advertising campaign) have been convinced that medications will cure sex problems, especially erectile dysfunction. Medication can be a valuable resource, but for the great majority of people medication is not effective as a stand-alone intervention (Kleinplatz, 2010). You need to address psychological, bio-medical, and social/relational factors for real and sustainable sexual change. Otherwise, the sexual problem becomes chronic and severe, undermining your relationship. You cannot treat sexual problems with benign neglect, they do not spontaneously get better. When treated with avoidance it is "the elephant in the room".

The most common sexual problem is low desire. A no sex relationship means the couple have intercourse less than ten times a year (less than once a month). This includes one in five marriages (and an even larger number of partnered and cohabitating couples). The pattern of sexual avoidance involves not just intercourse, but also sensual, playful, and erotic touch. Rather than touching and sexuality being energizing, sex problems have a major negative role which is destructive for your entire relationship.

It is worthwhile to challenge and change the negative role of sex, whether caused by psychological, bio-medical, or social/relational factors, whilst taking into account whether the sexual problem involves dysfunction, conflict over affairs, sexual secrets, sexual resentment, or sexual avoidance.

You need to confront the negative sexual factors as well as build healthy individual and couple sexuality. Changing the sexual "poisons" is necessary, but not sufficient. Rebuilding sexuality is necessary so it has a healthy role in your life and relationship.

## Brianne and Mark

Brianne and Mark have wonderful memories of their romantic love/passionate sex (limerance) phase. As well, they have good feelings about their 12 years as a married couple. This was dramatically altered four years ago when Brianne found that Mark had a secret sexual life of visiting prostitutes every six weeks to receive oral sex. At first Mark denied that this was an extra-marital affair (EMA) because he didn't have intercourse and there was no emotional connection with the women. Brianne said of course it was an EMA—he received oral sex and paid $100-$150. Sadly, Mark and Brianne fell into the typical EMA power struggle where the involved partner (Mark) claimed the injured partner (Brianne) was over-reacting and making a big deal of what was just a sexual dalliance. Brianne felt betrayed and negated, saying Mark was a sex addict, misused family funds, and negated her experience of giving oral sex because she wasn't a $150 woman. Nobody wins a power struggle, it is about not losing and feeling like the "bad spouse".

The individual therapists each spouse consulted gave confusing and contradictory advice. Brianne's therapist said Mark (whom she had not met) was a sex addict and Brianne was advised to consult a divorce attorney and give Mark an ultimatum. The therapist Mark consulted suggested he do something to atone for the EMA. The clinician suggested buying Brianne a gift to compensate for the money spent, agree to stop EMAs if she gave more oral sex, and for Mark to give more oral sex himself. These interventions reinforced emotional "heat" without shedding psychological "light".

Finally, at Brianne's urging, they consulted a couple therapist with an expertise in sexual problems. The first session was scheduled as a couple with the rationale that an EMA, like intimacy and sexuality, is best treated as a couple issue. In an empathic, respectful, yet confrontative manner the therapist made it clear that the attack—blame power struggle—had to stop. Their challenge was to make genuine meaning (a narrative about the EMA that both Brianne and Mark could accept). Each partner scheduled an individual psychological/relational/sexual history session to explore strengths and vulnerabilities. The fourth session was a 90-minute couple feedback session to (1) create a new, genuine narrative which included the EMA from the perspective of the injured and involved partner; (2) agree to a therapeutic contract for a 6-month good faith effort to create a healthy marriage and a new couple sexual style; and (3) begin the couple psychosexual skill exercises to engage in at home to build strong, resilient sexual desire. In addition, they would develop a new trust agreement and a plan to prevent an EMA in the future. These are couple challenges. You can learn from the past and honor these learnings, but you cannot undo the EMA or the pain caused by it. Brianne and Mark needed to establish a new, clear trust agreement, a new couple sexual style, and value their marriage, especially the role of intimacy and sexuality. Mark reinforced the insight that the power for change is in the present and future. Mark recognized that he made himself vulnerable to an EMA by de-eroticizing Brianne and their relationship. He'd treated marital sex with benign neglect. Sex was mechanical, with low satisfaction and without vitality. Mark recommitted to marital sexuality emphasizing desire/pleasure/eroticism/satisfaction. Sex would have a valued 15–20% role in his life and their marriage.

You cannot compare EMA sex with marital sex. EMA sex is like the limerance phase multiplied by three (secrecy, longing, and broken boundaries enhance erotic feelings). The empowering comparison is couple sex after treatment compared to couple sex before the EMA. Sexual recovery is a crucial component in the therapy.

Brianne was ambivalent about developing a new couple sexual style. On one hand, she felt that the inclusion of sensual, playful, and erotic sexuality would increase anticipation and enjoyment. Feeling that Mark valued eroticism with her and that he recognized her preferred erotic scenarios made sexuality vital and satisfying. She valued taking turns giving and receiving oral stimulation rather than their old pattern of mutual oral sex, which had raised self-consciousness and reduced sexual responsivity. In their new couple sexual style, Brianne felt desired as an erotic woman with eroticism integrated in couple sexuality.

Her ambivalence was that the new couple sexual style felt like rewarding Mark for the EMA. The therapist made it clear that the EMA and couple sexuality were two very separate issues. They took pride in being a resilient couple who developed a new sexual style so that sexuality had a positive role of energizing their bond. Both Brianne and Mark felt desire and desirable as erotic partners.

As a couple, they needed to confront the poisonous role of Mark's EMA. It was his EMA, so he needed to take responsibility for it. This included honoring both positive and negative learnings from the EMA.

Mark's positive learnings were that he valued eroticism, the security of his marriage, and that he could take emotional and sexual risks with Brianne. His negative learnings were that he had emotionally betrayed Brianne, that a secret sexual life was harmful to his marriage, and that the EMA stole time, money, and energy from his family.

Brianne needed to address her positive and negative learnings from the EMA. The EMA was not her fault or responsibility, but there were important learnings she could apply in the present and future. The most important positive learnings were she wanted a genuine loving relationship, to put more of herself into marital sexuality, and be a positive sexuality educator for her children. Negative learnings were she had avoided emotional issues with Mark—instead complaining to friends. She'd allowed herself and her marriage to slip into mediocre sexual habits. She now realized she had the right to make erotic requests.

The message to the couple was to put time, communication, and energy into their sexual relationship so it maintained a positive role. Just as importantly, they needed to confront and change negative sexual attitudes, behaviors, and emotions so these did not subvert their lives and relationship.

Dealing with the EMA was an opportunity to address sexual "poisons" and create a vital, satisfying couple sexuality. Prevention is always the better strategy, but as the EMA had happened, they needed to deal with reality, not "what could have been or should have been". Mark regretted the EMA and was committed to not repeat it. More important was his commitment to intimacy and eroticism with Brianne. When there were disappointments, frustrations, or conflicts, Mark would problem-solve with Brianne. He valued both a genuine sexual bond and a satisfying and secure relationship.

They developed a relapse prevention plan to ensure their marriage remained satisfying, secure, and sexual. This included scheduling six-monthly follow-up therapy sessions for two years. If they experienced a problem, they would call for a "booster session". The follow-up sessions reinforced gains and they set a growth goal for the next six months.

## Two Exercises to Implement Strategies to Confront the Sexual Paradox

The first exercise is to ensure that sexuality has a positive role in your life and relationship. Do this exercise alone first and then with your partner. In the individual phase, be honest with yourself in assessing past and present sexual attitudes, behaviors, and emotions. Be specific about positive sexual learnings and experiences. What were these learnings and who did you learn them from—parents, siblings, friends, school, religion? Do these still hold true in your life? When did you feel best about sensual and sexual touch? Were your experiences with self-exploration/masturbation positive? Most people, male and female, have their first orgasmic experience by themselves. Did this help you "own" your sexuality? Was sexuality your friend to be honored and valued? Share attitudes, experiences, values, and emotions about touch and sexuality with your partner.

Next, share positive learnings about relational sexuality, especially experiences with each other. Be aware of sensitivities regarding previous sexual relationships. Stay away from details and stories about other partners. This leads to unnecessary drama. It is worthwhile to share the themes of other partner sexual experiences. Did intimacy, pleasure-oriented touch, and sexuality enhance your relational development? Identify positive learnings which facilitate sexuality in your present life and relationship. Do not make comparisons with other people and experiences. Own your history and learnings.

Focus on sexual self-esteem. Do you feel you deserve sexuality to have a positive role in your life? Can you accept yourself with your psychological, relational, and sexual strengths and vulnerabilities? Do you anticipate touching and sexuality? Do you have the right to say "no" to sex, and freedom to say "yes"? Do you use effective contraception and practice safe sex? Does sexuality have a positive role in your life and relationship?

Have you and your partner developed a couple sexual style that is the right fit? Does your sexual style honor your unique "sexual voice" and allow you to be intimate and erotic allies so that desire is strong and resilient? Do you value both mutual, synchronous sexual experiences as well as asynchronous sexual encounters? Do both of you value intimacy and eroticism? Do you accept that sexuality can have a range of roles, meanings, and outcomes? When there is a disappointing, dissatisfying, or dysfunctional sexual experience do you accept this and turn toward each other? Is sexuality a shared pleasure, a means to reinforce intimacy, a tension reducer, and does it energize your bond? Do you embrace anti-perfectionism and anti-performance? Do you value real life couple sexuality? Remember, sexuality is not the primary factor in your relationship, but does play an integral 15–20% role.

The second exercise focuses on confronting and changing the destructive role of sexuality. The core issue from the past is shame. Shame causes a contingent sexual self-esteem. The key is acceptance of your sexual past. You can learn from the past, but you can't change the past. Your power for sexual change is in the present and future. Process and honor your learnings from the past, but do not give them control over your sexual self-esteem. Having regrets about the past is normal, but it is poisonous to feel shame. Whether sharing issues with your partner, best friend, minster, therapist, or journaling, you can process and learn from your sexual past. Regrets and sadness are normal and promote healing; shame has no value and keeps you stuck in the past.

A common negative factor is power struggles about past problems. Whether the issue was an EMA, denying the impact of sex dysfunction, struggles with infertility, an unwanted pregnancy, a secret sexual life, or arguing about a sexual encounter, almost all couples have at least one (and usually more) negative, confusing, guilt-inducing, or traumatic sexual experience. The challenge is to make genuine meaning of these experiences so they no longer have a destructive role in your life and relationship. The fall-out from the negative experience is more harmful than the experience itself. It is unhealthy when the couple say an EMA was the most important thing in their entire relationship or that resentment over dysfunctional sex controls them. A favorite adage is "Living well is the best revenge". Psychological, relational, and sexual well-being is promoted in the present; don't allow sexuality to be controlled by the past.

Be specific about what factors subvert couple sexuality. Which of these are resolvable, which modifiable, and which need to be accepted and worked around? A pervasive myth is "If you loved me we could resolve everything and have a perfect life". In truth, about 30% of problems are resolvable, 50–60% are modifiable, and even for the most loving relationships 10–20% of problems are unchangeable and need to be accepted (Gottman & Silver, 2015). Enjoy healthy sexuality for who your partner and relationship really are rather than an unrealistic, romantic love image. Love, communication, and attraction are valuable, but not magical. Positive, realistic expectations of your partner and relationship enhance satisfaction. This will not succeed as a novel, love song, or movie, but is the basis for healthy individual and couple sexuality.

## Summary

Our approach to the sexual paradox is the opposite of the "common sense" belief regarding the magic of loving communication and sexual attraction. Rather than sex being the major factor, healthy sexuality has a small, integral role in your life and relationship. The core of a relationship is a respectful, trusting, emotional commitment based on a positive influence process. The 15–20% role of sexuality is to energize your bond and reinforce feelings of desire and desirability. Healthy sexuality involves sexual self-esteem and being a sexual team who are intimate and erotic friends.

The sexual paradox is that destructive sexuality has the power to subvert your life and destroy your relationship. Sexual problems, dysfunction, conflicts, and avoidance have more power than the positive role of healthy sexuality. Build healthy individual and couple sexuality as well as confronting the "poisons" which subvert sexual self-esteem and undermine couple sexuality. Just creating healthy sexuality is not enough. You must address both positive and negative factors whether in the past or present. You deserve to experience the 15–20% role of healthy sexuality.

# 11

# VULNERABILITIES AND CHALLENGES

As you age and mature your sexual relationship can and should change. A foundation for healthy sexuality is maintaining your sexual voice (autonomy) based on self-acceptance. Acceptance is the core of being a sexual person and a sexual couple. Be open to your sexual changes, your partner's sexual changes, and growing as a sexual couple. Contrary to media myths of the joys of youthful sex, sexual satisfaction increases with age (Lindau et al., 2007).

We explore couple sexuality in adulthood—from 25 to 65. We offer guidelines rather than rigid rules in recognition of the diversity and complexity of people and relationships. A crucial guideline is "sexually, one size never fits all". We explore sexual vulnerabilities and challenges common to specific life phases and decisions. The overriding guideline is to establish a satisfying, secure, and sexual relationship. Sexuality has a 15–20% role—to energize your bond and reinforce feelings of desire and desirability at each life phase. We arbitrarily set age boundaries: 25–35, 35–45, 45–55, and 55–65. For example, the common challenge for 25–35 is to develop a couple sexual style and decide whether to have children. However, developing a couple sexual style is a challenge for a second marriage with people in their 50s, including dealing with the realities of young adult children from previous relationships.

## Vulnerabilities and Challenges: Ages 25–35

Most couples marry in their mid-20s to early/mid 30s. Very few people are virgins at marriage. You have established your life and sexual self-esteem. The challenge is to become an intimate sexual couple. This is a particularly vulnerable time for your relationship.

Most (not all) couples begin in a romantic love/passionate sex/idealized manner—the limerence phase (Tennov, 1998). We are fans of the limerance experience. However, it is crucial to realize this is a fragile, time-limited sexual phase—typically lasting six months to two years. A value of limerance is giving you the courage to commit to marriage (or a life partnership).

The challenge is to create a couple sexual style to reinforce desire/pleasure/eroticism/satisfaction. One of the saddest statistics is that 40% of couples say their best sex was in the first six months of the relationship. They did not develop a couple sexual style to maintain strong, resilient sexual desire.

For most couples, their relational style and their sexual style are different (McCarthy & Ross, 2017). This is a core concept, but not widely known. Couple relational style refers to how you deal with differences and conflicts. Couple sexual style refers to each partner having your "sexual voice" (autonomy) while being an intimate sexual team. The second factor is how the couple integrate intimacy and eroticism.

There is not a "right" relational style which fits all couples. The Best Friend relational style is the best fit for most couples. This style facilitates creating a respectful, trusting, emotionally intimate relationship. You trust there is a secure bond and that your partner "has your back". There will be differences and conflicts, but your partner would not do something to purposefully hurt or undercut you. Conflicts and hurt feelings do not degenerate into destructive power struggles. You value your partner and your bond.

Best Friend sexual style is not a good fit for most couples. The trap is there is so much closeness and emphasis on mutuality that you de-eroticize your partner and the relationship. For most couples a better decision is to adopt the Complementary couple sexual style. Engage in a dialogue about your preferred sexual style. Making a wise decision about sexuality and its role in your marriage (relationship) is a core challenge for this life phase.

A second crucial couple decision is whether to have children. If the answer is yes, how many children and the spacing of years between them. This is the life decision which is the hardest to change—career, money, where to live, marriage—all are easier to reverse than the decision about children. Whether your child is 3 or 10, it is emotionally gut-wrenching to decide you should be childless. Parenting is at least an 18-year (usually a lifetime) commitment.

This is not a "right—wrong" decision. Many couples thrive with children while others thrive with the decision to remain childless. For some couples, the "one and done" option is best while others prefer a family with between three and five children. This decision is typically made between 25–35. For couples over 35, sterilization is the most common method of birth control. Usually it is the woman who decides on a tubal ligation, because she has had as many children as she wants.

Ideally, the decision regarding children is positively motivated. Couples should use effective contraception until they decide to have a planned, wanted child. Unfortunately, that is not the norm. A significant number of pregnancies are unplanned, although this does not mean the child is unwanted. The scientific guideline is to wait at least two years after marriage to have a child. The rationale is it gives you time to do the challenging work of a new marriage—to create a respectful, trusting, emotionally committed relationship and develop a couple sexual style to replace the limerance phase (McCarthy & McCarthy, 2014). When couples wait until their mid to late 20s to marry this guideline makes sense. However, the guideline is not applicable for couples marrying in their mid to late 30s. As age increases so does the possibility of fertility problems. Infertility is devastating for the relationship and couple sexuality. Also, be aware of the opposite challenge; couples who have children or are pregnant before marriage. These diverse factors make it clear why we speak of guidelines rather than rules that apply to all people and all circumstances.

The challenge for couples with children is to maintain healthy sexuality while parenting. For 70% of couples, sexual frequency and satisfaction goes down at the birth of a first child and does not rebound until the last child leaves home. For most, the "empty nest" syndrome is a misnomer. The "couple again" phase is one of renewed relational and sexual satisfaction (Pascoal et al., 2017).

A common vulnerability is lowered sexual frequency and satisfaction. This is due to the reality that the early years of marriage require work; very different than "happy ever after" myths. This is the time that marriages are most likely to end. Of couples who eventually divorce, almost 40% of divorces occur in the first five years of marriage. The rate of relationship breakup is even higher for partnered and cohabitating couples (Finkel, 2017).

Couples who thrive between 25–35 create a solid foundation for the marriage with sexuality having an integral, 15–20% role of energizing their bond and promoting feelings of desire and desirability. Develop a couple sexual style which promotes desire/pleasure/eroticism/satisfaction. You make a decision about couple sexuality and family and are ready for your challenges during ages 35–45.

## Vulnerabilities and Challenges: Ages 35–45

In this life stage, the vulnerability is settling for a mediocre, predictable sexual relationship, with sex relegated to a late-night routine after everything is taken care of. The challenge is to maintain a vital, satisfying sexual relationship and value being a couple rather than sexuality subverted by work, parenting, household, and life.

Maintaining a vital, satisfying sexuality involves valuing intimacy and security while remaining open to exploration and growth. Sexually you cannot rest on your laurels. Healthy sexuality requires thought, dialogue, energy, and willingness to explore sexual scenarios and techniques. So many couples fall into the pattern of sex on a weekend night after the children are asleep. Even if sex remains functional, the predictable routine of five minutes of foreplay, three minutes of intercourse, and two minutes of afterplay does not reinforce desire and satisfaction. Sexual desire is facilitated by positive anticipation, pleasure-oriented touching, freedom and choice of sexual expression, and unpredictability.

Routine, mechanical sex subverts desire. Sex as a performance pressure or coercion kills desire. The traditional male—female power struggle over intercourse frequency poisons desire. The antidote is engaging in pleasure-oriented touching inside and outside your bedroom with the understanding that touching has value for itself. Enjoy affectionate, sensual, playful, and erotic touch in addition to intercourse. Both partners value intimacy and eroticism rather than being split by traditional gender roles.

Increase awareness of the multiple roles, meanings, and outcomes of couple sexuality. Ideally, this involves embracing Good Enough Sex (GES) rather than expecting each sexual encounter to be mutual, synchronous, and energizing. Unfortunately, accepting GES usually does not occur until later in your relationship. The man insists on the need to ensure each encounter includes erection, intercourse, and ejaculation (we will discuss this challenge in detail in the 45–55 age section). It is crucial in maintaining satisfying sexuality to accept a range of sexual outcomes from dynamite to dysfunctional. Even when the sexual experience is mediocre, dissatisfying, or dysfunctional, turn toward your partner rather than feeling guilty or blaming. Affirm that the best sex is mutual and synchronous. However, the majority of sexual encounters are asynchronous. This is healthy as long as it's not at the expense of your partner or relationship.

Sometimes sex is about sharing pleasure, sometimes sex is a tension reducer, sometimes sex is to liven up a boring day, sometimes sex is lustful and dramatic, sometimes sex is to share intimacy or a tender moment, sometimes sex is to express sadness, sometimes sex is to reconnect or make-up, sometimes sex is one way and selfish, sometimes sex is a playful way to be together. Couples who recognize that sexuality can have a number of roles and meanings, including different meanings for each partner, have a strong, resilient sexual relationship.

The second challenge is to make room for couple sexuality in the busyness of parenting, career, household, activities, family, and social responsibilities. Don't fall into the habit of late night sex after everything else is taken care of. Quality sexuality requires you to be awake and aware. Most sexual encounters are planned or semi-planned. If all sex had to be spontaneous and passionate, there would be much less sex. Sex is more frequent and satisfying on vacation because there is greater opportunity and less stress. Few couples prefer late night sex. Being sexual before or after a nap, in the guest room or family room, in front of a fireplace or on the porch, can be special and inviting. A key to sexual desire is freedom and unpredictability.

With children, whether toddlers or adolescents, their feelings and needs are immediate and can overwhelm adult needs, especially your need for intimate couple time. Yet, one of the best investments you make to ensure healthy, secure children is a healthy marriage and stable family. Children knowing you are an affectionate couple is reassuring even if they joke you're being "yucky". However, sex in front of children breaks boundaries—it is confusing and intimidating for the child. Be an "askable" parent when it comes to sex education and sexuality issues. Obviously, sexual explicitness is different for a 4-year-old than a 14-year-old. What doesn't change is the basic message that sex is good, not bad; that sexuality is integral to being a female or a male; and that you are there for your child whether as a sexuality educator or dealing with sexual problems. A valuable guideline is "Never lie to your children about sex". It is normal to say, "I can't talk to you about this now, but will when you are older". As adults, people complain mightily that their parents would avoid sexual topics or only speak about negatives like unplanned pregnancies, STI/HIV, and sexual trauma. These issues need to be addressed, but don't begin sex education with a negative. Begin with clear, positive sexual words and affirmative attitudes toward touch and pleasure. It's a one—two approach of sex education/positive sexuality first and confronting sexual problems and conflicts second.

For 70% of couples, sexual frequency and satisfaction goes down at the birth of a first child and doesn't rebound until the last child leaves. That's not healthy for you, your partner, your relationship, or your family. Balancing your life, parenting, relationship, and sexuality is a challenge, but a challenge worth meeting.

Is it possible to be a positive sex educator for your children if your sexual life is conflictual or dysfunctional? Yes. You owe it to your children to be a positive sex educator even if you are not a positive model. Good parenting does not mean pretending that everything is perfect. Remember, don't lie to your children. We are all human, with psychological, relational, and sexual vulnerabilities.

Couples complain they are too tired and don't have the time to be sexual. Our answer is to ask about your favorite TV show—which people love talking about. If you have time to watch a 30 or 60-minute show once a week you have time to be sexual. The typical sexual scenario is between 15–45 minutes, of which three to nine minutes involve intercourse. Of course, couples have two-minute "quickies" as well as two-hour lovemaking experiences. Set aside time when both partners are receptive and responsive to a sexual encounter whether synchronous or asynchronous. When sex occurs less than twice a month it adds to self-consciousness and performance pressure. Sexuality can be an integral part of your couple life with a range of roles, meanings, and outcomes. This affirms the value of intimacy and sexuality. Your life need not be controlled by work, parenting, household chores, and social and family responsibilities. In the balancing act of life, you want sexual time to nurture and energize your relationship. Sexuality can play a positive role in your hectic life.

**Vulnerabilities and Challenges: Ages 45–55**

For many couples, this is a time of sexual growth and satisfaction. The challenges are entering the "couple again" phase and adopting the Good Enough Sex (GES) model. The vulnerabilities are launching children and dealing with less predictable sexual response. This is a time of potential sexual growth as well as vulnerabilities.

Some couples enter the "couple again" phase in their late 30s and others not until their late 60s (for couples who are childless this is not a relevant dimension). It is crucial to meet the important challenge of being a couple again. Adolescent children are often stressful for their parents. Parenting is less labor intensive, but there are heightened fears and less control. "Little children, little problems, big children, big problems". For many adolescents, 13–16 is the most unsettling time in life, which makes it stressful for parents. Couples who understand that the most important bond in the family is the husband—wife bond (where sexuality joins you) do better individually, relationally, and parentally. Adolescent children often push boundaries, which makes the adults feel vulnerable. This is true whether you are in a traditional first marriage, a blended family, or a different family arrangement. Being a parental team and an intimate sexual team presents practical and emotional challenges.

Throughout childhood, middle school, and high school the adult role is to be a positive sexuality educator. "Knowledge is power". You want your child to be knowledgeable about both the positive aspects of sexuality and sexual problems (abuse, STI/HIV, unwanted pregnancy). Adolescent and young adult sexuality are among the most challenging times. You want your children to develop at their pace, not feel pressured or coerced. Being an "askable" parent is important. Parents become more sexually conservative with their adolescent and young adult children because of fear of negative sexual consequences. It is a balancing act of being a positive sex person/educator with a realistic awareness of potential sexual problems adolescents encounter. Being a pro-sexual person and a positive couple model is helpful for your adolescent and young adult children.

Being a couple again can be revitalizing personally, relationally, and sexually. It provides the opportunity to accept your sexual history with its strengths and vulnerabilities. Very few people reach age 55 without some bad or sad psychological, relational, or sexual experiences. Negative sexual experiences are part of being a person and couple. Rather than feeling secretive or shameful, you (with your partner's support) can accept the past. You cannot change the past; your power for change is in the present and future.

Reinforce desire/pleasure/eroticism/satisfaction in the couple again phase. Many couples are burdened by negative feelings, especially anger and resentment. These can include a range of incidents from sexual dalliances or affairs, blaming or shaming the partner, sexual dysfunction or avoidance, an STI or pregnancy, being caught in family secrets or feuds, struggles over masturbation or porn use, and keeping sensitive information from the partner. A genuine apology is helpful and healing. More important is a commitment to live your lives in the present and future in an emotionally and sexually healthy manner.

As a couple again, you have the time and space to establish a new balance for your personal, relational, and sexual lives. An example is taking advantage of privacy. You can be sexual before or after a weekend nap or have sex in the living or dining room where you don't fear an interruption (close the shades). Redecorate your bedroom and/or add a lounging chair as a sexual cue. Energy which went into parenting can now turn into couple energy. Interestingly, when couples are given the choice of when to be sexual few choose late at night. When is your favorite time to be sexual—when you wake, after a cup of coffee, after a shower so you are fresh for oral sex, before or after a nap, before dinner (sex as an appetizer) or after dinner (sex as dessert)? Being a couple again allows you to take a weekend trip. Do you prefer a hotel with a spa, camping under the stars, or a historic inn as a cue for sexuality? Take advantage of sexual freedom and opportunities.

Young couples settle into a sexual script where the man initiates with a spontaneous erection. Hopefully, she is sexually receptive and responsive so they enjoy a mutual, synchronous sexual experience. Often, the sex is better for him than her. Both assume sex will be predictable and functional for him.

A major vulnerability, especially for males 45 and older, is that totally predictable erections and intercourse become variable and flexible. Although male friends do not talk about this, by age 45 most men have had at least one experience where they don't get or maintain an erection sufficient for intercourse. So, a dreaded male fear is an almost universal experience. Not having an erection resulting in intercourse does not mean you have erectile dysfunction (ED). ED is a chronic sexual dysfunction which can be caused by a combination of psychological, bio-medical, and social/relational factors. Once you have a "sensitizing" experience, you seldom return to autonomous sex function.

You can become a better lover and enjoy couple sexuality if you accept that sex is more than intercourse. With aging, sex becomes more of a team sport. You need your partner as your intimate and erotic ally. Intimate, interactive couple sexuality is more satisfying than autonomous sex performance. It is a challenge to embrace a variable, flexible pleasure-oriented couple approach, but a very worthwhile learning. Your partner wants you to be her intimate and erotic friend rather than distracted by performance anxiety. You are present during the sexual encounter and enjoy giving and receiving pleasure-oriented touching rather than approaching sex as a pass—fail performance test.

A major mistake middle-years men make is rushing to intercourse as soon as they become erect. Think of subjective arousal on a 10-point scale: 0=neutral, 4–5=beginning arousal, 8=erotic flow, and 10=orgasm. Remember two important guidelines. First, subjective arousal is more important than objective arousal. Feeling "turned-on" is more important than an erection (or vaginal lubrication). When you focus on receptivity and responsivity to pleasure, objective arousal will follow. If you try to force arousal, both subjective and objective arousal are subverted. Second, do not rush intercourse. Transition to intercourse when your subjective arousal is an "8" (at least a "7"). The major reason men fail with Viagra is they rush to intercourse as soon as they are erect rather than transitioning to intercourse when they are into an erotic flow. For women, intercourse is more inviting when they feel receptive and responsive to genital stimulation—subjective arousal "8" rather than as soon as he thinks she's "ready".

GES is a couple process focused on sharing pleasure, not sex as an individual pass—fail performance. Perhaps 85% of sexual encounters involve awareness, comfort, pleasure, arousal, erotic flow, intercourse, and orgasm. The key in embracing GES is to welcome sexual variability and flexibility rather than panic and blame when sexuality does not flow. GES recognizes that sensual, playful, and erotic scenarios are sexual. If sex does not flow to intercourse, you can enjoy synchronous or asynchronous sensual, playful, or erotic experiences.

Women find GES easier to accept because it is congruent with their lived sexual experiences. Women embrace variable, flexible, couple sexuality. This is a challenge to the man's performance orientation. Yet, it is acceptance of GES that allows him to be sexual in his 60s, 70s, and 80s. Traditional men stop being sexual because of frustration and embarrassment, which leads to sexual avoidance. Implementing GES during the 45–55 phase allows you to enjoy lifelong sexuality.

### Vulnerabilities and Challenges: Ages 55–65

The 55–65 age range can be a very vulnerable time sexually for individuals and couples. Your vascular, neurological, and hormonal systems are less strong so psychological, relational, and psychosexual skill factors become more important. With aging, you need each other as intimate and erotic friends. The old belief was that sex is less frequent and intense so it's less meaningful. This myth cheats the aging couple of sexual pleasure and satisfaction.

The core challenges between 55–65 are to establish a solid foundation for lifelong sexual intimacy and to embrace a broad-based sexual repertoire which facilitates desire/pleasure/eroticism/satisfaction.

The traditional couple have been together between 25–40 years. The vulnerability is staying with what you know and not taking emotional or sexual risks. Enjoy the foundation of intimacy and security and use that as a launching pad to add sexual playfulness, eroticism, and vitality. Sexual satisfaction can increase with age. Maintain a balance between security and exploration, between acceptance and taking risks. Share and explore new understandings, feelings, scenarios, and techniques. A value in a long-term relationship is if you take a sexual risk and it is awkward or a dud, you don't fear humiliation by your partner. When trying sexual scenarios and techniques there are no guarantees. We hate popular magazines and websites that guarantee a sex technique will work for all people. They are lying to you. An example is saying all women love oral stimulation with the man's tongue swirling around the woman's clitoris. Many women find that highly erotic, while others feel it's a turn-off. Or that all men enjoy "deep throat" fellatio. A significant group of men who enjoy manual sex and intercourse find receiving oral sex a turn-off. What are you willing to try with the hope it will build eroticism for you personally and as a couple?

Each partner has preferred pleasuring techniques, preferred erotic techniques, preferred intercourse techniques, preferred ways to be orgasmic, and preferred afterplay techniques. As you age you become your own sexual person as well as an intimate sexual partner. You are not sexual clones of each other. The more you accept your authentic sexual self, the stronger is couple sexuality.

A core factor is your approach to intercourse. Intercourse is a routine part of most couple's sexual repertoire, almost automatic. Even for the one in three women who are not orgasmic during intercourse, there is something predictable and "normal" about intercourse. Couples between

55–65 enjoy intercourse and accept that sensual, playful, and erotic scenarios are sexual—don't fall into the intercourse or nothing trap. This is the right life phase to embrace GES, partly because it establishes the foundation for being sexual in your 70s and 80s. Prevention is always a good strategy whether for your health, relationship, or sexuality. This gives you the opportunity to build a solid foundation for sexuality during your senior years.

The second major challenge is to create a broad-based sexual repertoire which facilitates couple sexuality. Valuing variable, flexible sexuality rather than routine, predictable intercourse is the guiding strategy. Become comfortable and confident with a broad sexual repertoire which values sensual, playful, and erotic scenarios. This is particularly important when the sexual experience does not flow to intercourse. Broad-based couple sexuality is valuable for itself. Couples feel awkward the first time the partner says let's have a sensual date or an erotic date. Practice this two to four times to see whether it fits your sexual repertoire. Having several ways to connect and reconnect sexually is an empowering couple resource.

Genuinely embrace GES. Turn toward your partner whether it was a wonderful, vital sexual encounter or a dissatisfying or dysfunctional encounter. This ensures sexuality will continue to be part of your real-life couple experience.

Most couples use the partner interaction arousal/eroticism. This is the type of sex you see in movies and read about in novels—one partner's sexual responsiveness plays off the other's. The best aphrodisiac is an involved, aroused partner. Utilize partner interaction arousal/eroticism throughout your relationship.

The second most common arousal/eroticism pattern is self-entrancement arousal. It follows the classic sensate focus experience where one partner is the giver and the other the receiver. Your goal as the giver is not to turn-on your partner, but to touch for yourself, providing you enjoy giving (Weiner & Avery-Clark, 2017). The receiver is not passive, but aware and mindful. The receiver is actively involved in sensations and feelings of pleasure. You take turns, but not necessarily in the same session. Often, self-entrancement arousal is asynchronous. The experience can proceed to orgasm, but that is not a demand. The special value of self-entrancement arousal is it facilitates a variable, flexible sexual repertoire. Use of self-entrancement arousal increases with age.

The third arousal/eroticism pattern is role enactment arousal. This is the most challenging and contentious pattern. For some couples role enactment is highly valued while for others it is intimidating and a turn-off. Role enactment arousal features external stimuli to eroticize your relationship. This can include reading erotic stories, watching an X-rated video, using sexual toys like blindfolds or handcuffs, playing out an erotic fantasy, or being sexual in front of a mirror. Role enactment arousal is featured on the internet and sex magazines, but is the least utilized arousal/eroticism pattern. Couples who value role enactment arousal feel it frees them and adds an erotic charge. You can embrace role enactment arousal, use it on special occasions, or decide to skip it and enjoy partner interaction and self-entrancement arousal/eroticism.

The balance between intimacy/security and exploring/sexual risks will vary between partners and within couples. You can create a variable, flexible repertoire that reinforces couple sexuality with aging.

## Couple Exercise: Vulnerabilities and Challenges

To make the concept of vulnerabilities and challenges personal and concrete we ask you to honestly examine your relationship. What are your couple vulnerabilities and challenges at this time? More important than your age, identify personally relevant vulnerabilities and challenges.

We encourage you to write a letter to your partner. Start with challenges you have successfully met and then spell out the specific vulnerabilities you are now feeling personally and as a couple. Next, what do you need to do, what are you requesting your partner do, and what do you need as a couple to meet this challenge? Each person reads their letter out loud. The partner listens and takes it in. Do not be defensive or counter argue. Be sure you understand each other's feelings and especially the sexual requests.

After you have processed each letter, focus on your couple challenge and growth strategy to enhance your sexual relationship. Remember, this is not a performance or to prove something. Focus on exploring and sharing so you meet the challenge and enhance desire/pleasure/eroticism/satisfaction.

We suggest follow-up dialogues on a yearly basis to ensure relational and sexual changes are worthwhile and sustainable. A core issue in a healthy relationship is a positive influence process and working as an intimate sexual team.

## Estella and Avery

Estella and Avery were a couple for three years when they married at the average age of their cohort—26 for Estella and 28 for Avery. They cohabitated for 19 months and believed the transition to marriage would be seamless. They were surprised to learn that this is a myth. Most couples cohabitate before marriage. Yet, they find the first two years of marriage challenging. Developing a respectful, trusting, emotionally committed marriage and a couple sexual style which promotes desire and satisfaction are crucial challenges.

Avery assumed that becoming pregnant would be easy. Estella had heard from female friends that getting pregnant could be difficult, so she was relieved that she became pregnant within two months. Sex with the goal of pregnancy was an aphrodisiac. The surprising challenge was being a sexual couple during pregnancy. Estella had two vulnerabilities she felt Avery did not appreciate. First, she did not enjoy hard-driving intercourse when pregnant. Second, the issue of intercourse positions during the last trimester. Estella believed Avery ignored these concerns. Avery wanted to remain a sexual couple during the pregnancy, but felt Estella was shy and not forthcoming about what she needed sexually. They were clear communicators and problem solvers, but not about sexual strategies and techniques.

They muddled through the first pregnancy. It took the second pregnancy to meet the challenge and enjoy sexuality throughout the pregnancy. What made the difference was using the sitting-kneeling intercourse position (Estella learned this in her prepared childbirth class) and using circular thrusting rather than rapid in—out thrusting. Avery was clear that he cared about making love with Estella, not just intercourse frequency. Estella had always enjoyed giving manual stimulation and during the pregnancy she increased comfort with giving and receiving oral stimulation. This time they enjoyed sexuality during pregnancy. This put them in a better position to address the vulnerability of balancing parenting with being a sexual couple.

They wanted to be in the 30% of couples who value satisfying sexuality while being parents. They realized there would be a diverse set of vulnerabilities and challenges in the years ahead. Avery and Estella were committed to a satisfying, secure, and sexual marriage and being sex educators for their children.

## Summary

As a relationship continues you experience different vulnerabilities and challenges. Some are predictable while others are totally unexpected. If the challenge is successfully met, your relationship is stronger, with increased efficacy in addressing future vulnerabilities and challenges. When a vulnerability is ignored, this makes you more vulnerable in the future.

Couples in a long-term first marriage find that their relationship has significantly changed over time. It is as if you've had three to four marriages, just to the same person. It is crucial to recognize sexual vulnerabilities and challenges. Couples go through stressful psychological, relational, and sexual times—it's a normal part of life and an intimate relationship. The key for survival is to not be controlled by negative cognitions and feelings from the past. The key for thriving is to continue touching even when you are feeling disappointed or upset. Remind each other that you are intimate and erotic friends and strive for a satisfying, secure, and sexual relationship.

# 12

# SEXUALITY AND AGING

There is solid scientific support for the value of couple sexuality in your 60s, 70s, and 80s. A prime factor in successful sexuality with aging is valuing intimacy, pleasure, and eroticism. An important understanding is that there is no illness or disability which destroys your need for touch or your sexual desire. Aging, illness, or disability can alter sexual function, but you still experience desire and satisfaction. Sexual satisfaction increases with aging, even as frequency and function become more variable. Take pride in "beating the odds" and recognize that with aging sexuality is more interactive, human, and genuine. You need each other as intimate and erotic allies in a way you hadn't 20 years before.

The essence of health sexuality is giving and receiving pleasure-oriented touch. Sexuality includes sensual, playful, and erotic touch as valuable for itself, not just building to intercourse. The man learns to piggy-back his arousal on hers. You need each other as intimate and erotic friends. Embrace Good Enough Sex (GES) and accept the multiple roles, meanings, and outcomes of sexuality. All the good learnings about sexuality come to fruition with your aging process (Metz & McCarthy, 2010).

The anticipation of sexual touch, feeling you deserve pleasure as you age, enjoying the "couple again" phase, taking advantage of freedom and choice with sensual, playful, and erotic scenarios, and embracing the challenges and unpredictability of couple sexuality, all serve to enhance your sexual experience. For the woman, realizing that the man needs her touch and sexual responsivity makes the sexual experience more involving, genuine, and satisfying. For the man, realizing that he has "beaten the odds" and is a "wise man" who turns toward his partner and adopts GES is motivating and empowering. Sexuality and aging is truly an intimate team process.

The bad news is that one in three couples stop being sexual between 60 and 65 and two in three between 70 and 75. Contrary to "common sense" beliefs, the decision to stop sex is made by the man. He has lost confidence with erection, intercourse, and orgasm. He feels anxious and humiliated and says to himself "I don't want to start something I can't finish". He makes the choice unilaterally and conveys it non-verbally by avoidance. He not only stops intercourse, but all types of sensual and sexual touch—sometimes even affectionate touch. The woman feels blamed and rejected. They remain together, but in a demoralized and often alienated manner. Rather than sexuality having a positive 15–20% role in their lives and relationship, it has a powerful draining role.

The fact that it's the man who chooses to stop sex is the opposite of the gender and media stereotypes. This adds to stigma and confusion, especially when he blames her for the sexual problem. Women, including those with a history of low desire, orgasmic dysfunction, or sexual pain, feel sad about the cessation of touch and sexual expression.

Sexuality with aging is a "wise decision" for the man, woman, and couple. Most men thrive after 65 with retirement, but as many as 30% "crash and burn" in terms of depression, alcohol abuse, and becoming the stereotypical "grumpy old man". A major predictor of crashing and burning is ceasing intercourse and other forms of sexual touch. It isn't just a sexual loss, but a negation of emotional connection and personal vitality. The choice to stop being sexual is self-defeating for the man, the relationship, and the family. Rather than sexuality having a positive role; it plays a destructive role for the man and couple. It is especially problematic when affectionate touch is stopped. The relationship survives, but in a demoralized and diminished manner.

## Core Concepts in Sexuality and Aging

The key to vital sexuality is to integrate intimacy, non-demand pleasuring, and erotic scenarios and techniques. This is true of all couples, but particularly important for aging couples. With aging, healthy couple sexuality reaches fruition.

You need each other to share pleasure and eroticism and to confront the individual sex performance pass—fail approach. Recognize the multiple roles, meanings, and outcomes of couple sexuality. When a sexual encounter is dissatisfying or dysfunctional, turn toward each other as intimate and erotic allies rather than blaming or avoiding.

With aging, your vascular, neurological, and hormonal systems are less efficient. This means that psychological, relational, and especially psychosexual skill factors become more important for sexual function. This includes using a vaginal lubricant prophylactically, spending more time with pleasuring, using self-entrancement arousal scenarios, adopting variable, flexible couple sexuality, enjoying sensual and erotic scenarios, "piggy-backing" his arousal on hers, valuing both planned and spontaneous sexual encounters, embracing GES, valuing both asynchronous and synchronous sexual experiences.

The sexual challenges for men include taking more time with pleasuring, being open to direct penile stimulation to build arousal, accepting erections not as firm and which wax and wane, and a lessened need to ejaculate at each sexual encounter. The biggest challenge is embracing GES as first class male sexuality and being the "wise" man who drops the traditional approach to erection and intercourse as a performance test. First class male sexuality is about sharing pleasure and turning toward your partner as your intimate and erotic friend.

The special challenges for women include emphasizing subjective rather than objective arousal, using a vaginal lubricant, taking time to build pleasure and arousal, accepting changes in your physical body including lessened orgasmic intensity, and valuing integrated, satisfying sexuality. Accepting that arousal and orgasm is easier for you than your partner enhances sexual pleasure and satisfaction.

Both women and men can use pro-sexuality medications as a resource. However, not as a stand-alone intervention. You cannot ask a medication to do more than it can do. If there are extremely low levels of testosterone, testosterone enhancement can be valuable for the woman and man. However, don't depend on testosterone to be the sole or prime resource for sexual desire. Viagra for men or Addyi for women is not successful as a stand-alone medication. The medical intervention needs to be integrated into your couple style of intimacy, pleasuring, and eroticism. A crucial factor is to adopt the couple-oriented GES model rather than expecting perfect individual sex performance. Do not compare sexuality in your 60s with sex in your 20s or your 40s. Accepting positive, realistic couple sexuality with its variability and flexibility is crucial for sexual satisfaction in your 60s, 70s, and 80s.

Sexuality is more than genitals, intercourse, and orgasm. Sexuality includes sensual, playful, and erotic touch. Not all touch can or should result in intercourse. Couples who adopt GES report high levels of satisfaction.

Self-acceptance, especially of your aging body, promotes partner acceptance. Emphasize the core role of giving and receiving pleasure-oriented touch. This is the key factor in promoting responsive sexual desire for both the woman and man. An involved, responsive partner is the major aphrodisiac.

Maintaining a regular rhythm of sexual contact is crucial. This means valuing affectionate, sensual, playful, erotic, and intercourse touch. When couples avoid touch or their only sexual touch is intercourse, self-consciousness and anxiety replace comfort and positive anticipation. A key to satisfying couple sexuality is to maintain pleasure-oriented connection which emphasizes a broad, flexible approach (Metz, Epstein & McCarthy, 2017).

Emphasize female—male equity and being an intimate sexual team. Couples who cling to the double standard are vulnerable to unsatisfying and dysfunctional sex. Appreciate and enjoy the gender role reversal. Female sexual response and orgasm become easier than male sexual response. He learns to "piggy-back" his arousal on hers, a crucial psychosexual skill with aging. Remember, sexuality is about sharing pleasure.

The woman chooses a lubricant that feels and smells sensual and utilizes it prophylactically to facilitate intercourse (rather than wait until she feels pain with intromission or during thrusting). Many women prefer to initiate intercourse when subjective arousal is high and guide intromission, since they are after all the experts on their own vaginas.

The man accepts and enjoys his mature penis. He should not compare this to the spontaneous, totally predictable erection of his 20s. The key to erectile comfort and confidence is physical and psychological relaxation. Enjoy your body, your partner's body, and your sexual experience rather than focusing narrowly on a firm erection and intercourse.

Replace the perfect intercourse performance model with GES. Eighty-five percent of encounters flow to intercourse. When sex does not flow, rather than apologize or panic, switch to an erotic scenario for both partners (synchronous) or one partner (asynchronous). Another alternative is a warm, sensual, cuddly scenario where you share sexuality in a sensual manner.

Sex after 65 is intimate, genuine, and human. Enjoy these feelings and sensations and turn toward each other as intimate and erotic allies. Remember, the core of sexuality is giving and receiving pleasure-oriented touching.

## Brenda and Gary

This was a second marriage for both Brenda and Gary. Brenda was 76, Gary 74, and they'd been a couple for 22 years. They began as a romantic love/passionate sex couple and had good memories of their 18 month limerance phase. The next 10–15 years of their relationship involved sex which was functional, but not energizing or special. In many ways, they were a Traditional sexual style couple where Gary emphasized intercourse and sex frequency, while Brenda felt she was "along for the ride". Like many women, Brenda found it easier to be orgasmic with manual or rubbing stimulation, but Gary wanted her to have a "real" orgasm during intercourse. Although she could be orgasmic during intercourse, Gary valued this more than Brenda. She would fake orgasm so he could let go and ejaculate. Gary enjoyed sex more than Brenda. Fortunately, sex was more of a positive than a problem in their lives.

This began changing as Gary entered his 60s. Erectile function became less reliable even though he regularly used Viagra. As soon as he became erect, Gary rushed to intercourse because he feared losing the erection. Sex was less fun for Brenda because she wasn't subjectively aroused. Even though she used a vaginal lubricant, intercourse was uncomfortable and sometimes painful. They joked about sex, but did not have an open dialogue about sexual strategies and techniques.

They fell into a pattern where Gary blamed his erection problems on Brenda's dry vagina and Brenda felt Gary was obsessive about his penis and intercourse. He ignored her feelings and pleasure. They no longer felt like an intimate sexual team. The definition of a low sex marriage is intercourse between 11–23 times a year, and this is the pattern Gary and Brenda were in.

It was Brenda who suggested they consult a couple therapist. Gary was a very reluctant client because he felt embarrassed. He wanted a medical answer—a pill, testosterone, or an injection so he could perform. The couple therapist had a specialty in sex therapy. She utilized a four-session assessment model with the first meeting as a couple to reinforce that sex problems are a couple issue. She then scheduled a psychological/relational/sexual history session with Gary and a separate session with Brenda. In the individual session, Gary disclosed that he masturbated ten times a month and had good erections. Gary expected to be blamed by the therapist and was surprised when she said the majority of married men masturbate and it was a good prognostic sign that he had good erections with masturbation. Like most men, Gary had limited knowledge of erections and sexual response. Gary was surprised to learn that the mechanism for Viagra was to relax the penile muscles so blood would flow and facilitate erection. When he masturbated, Gary was not anxious nor performance-oriented. He spent time on self-stimulation and erotic fantasy. He transitioned from pleasure to arousal to erotic flow to orgasm. With intercourse sex, he rushed the process, driven by fear of losing his erection. As soon as an erection began (subjective arousal of "4" on a "10" point scale) he tried to force intromission. The therapist suggested delaying intromission until subjective arousal was "8" or at least "7". She urged them to engage in multiple stimulation (giving and receiving) before and during intercourse. Gary used private erotic fantasies to enhance erotic flow.

The most important thing the therapist said to Gary was that whether it occurred once a month, once every ten times, or once a year, almost all men over 60 have at least one (usually more) unsuccessful intercourse experiences each year. Gary was urged to be a "wise" man and adopt GES. A wise man turns toward his partner as his intimate and erotic ally. You "beat the odds" and can enjoy sexuality in your 60s, 70s, and 80s.

In the individual session with Brenda, the therapist noted Brenda had lost her "sexual voice". She had been so reactive to Gary that she'd given up desire/pleasure/eroticism/satisfaction for herself. In trying not to pressure Gary, Brenda had stopped enjoying touching and eroticism. Brenda being pro-sexual was good for her and good for him and for their sexual relationship. This was a new, challenging way of thinking. Brenda's preferred "orgasmic voice" was with manual and rubbing stimulation which did not require a firm erection or intercourse. Her orgasmic pattern was normal and healthy, not a dysfunction—an empowering insight. Brenda wanted to be an active sexual partner rather than all the pressure being on Gary, who had isolated himself, hoping for a medical intervention to provide a guaranteed erection. With these new understandings, Brenda felt better about herself and sexuality than she had in years.

The 90-minute couple feedback session is core in this therapeutic model. To the surprise of both Gary and Brenda the therapist focused on desire as the core issue rather than ED. The first priority was to reestablish sexual comfort, attraction, and trust. They would anticipate touching and sexuality rather than dread it. Neither Brenda nor Gary felt they deserved pleasurable touch.

The desire psychosexual skill exercises are engaged in at home, beginning with comfort, with sensual and playful touch. The therapist did not place a prohibition on intercourse, but was clear that intercourse was not expected or demanded. Brenda took the lead in transitioning from sensual to playful to erotic touch. For years, Brenda had minimized the value of receiving manual stimulation or actively rubbing her vulva against Gary's body. Both Gary and Brenda were surprised how receptive and responsive she was to erotic stimulation. Rather than switching to intercourse, they enjoyed erotic stimulation to orgasm. This had not been part of their sexual repertoire for years. Gary was turned-on by Brenda's sexual responsiveness, rather than obsessing and being hyper-vigilant about his erection. This was the most sexual fun Gary had had in years.

The experience of Brenda being orgasmic with rubbing stimulation and Gary not having an orgasm was new. Brenda worried he'd feel cheated and resentful, and was surprised that Gary's reaction was positive. He felt turned-on by her sexual responsivity. He was reluctant to try intercourse because he feared a "failure". Gary hadn't had an orgasm outside of intercourse since adolescence.

At the next therapy session, the clinician noted that almost all men prefer to transition to intercourse on their first erection and to have orgasm during intercourse. This is a healthy preference, but a self-defeating mandate. Could Gary meet the challenge of enjoying orgasm with manual, oral, or rubbing stimulation? Brenda encouraged him to adopt a variable, flexible approach to sexual expression. Gary was ambivalent—this would reduce intercourse performance pressure, but he felt he was "less of a man" and "settling". Brenda assured Gary she would enjoy his erotic response, especially pleasuring him to orgasm.

Over the next two weeks, they had five sexual encounters—three involving erotic stimulation to orgasm and two involving intercourse. In four of the five Brenda was orgasmic with manual or rubbing stimulation. At the next therapy session, they discussed their experiences and feelings. Brenda had found her sexual voice and was clear about her desires. Her "orgasmic voice" was with erotic sexual expression. She wanted Gary to accept this as right for her. She enjoyed giving oral stimulation, but did not enjoy receiving oral sex. Gary was confused. He'd always heard that women felt cheated by not having orgasm during intercourse and that all women enjoyed cunnilingus. Brenda was assertive, saying as an aging woman she had a right to her sexual preferences, which involved erotic sexuality, but not cunnilingus. This openness made it easier for Gary to confront the narrow role of sex performance. As an aging man, Gary wanted to share sexuality with Brenda rather than perform for her. Gary's preference was for intercourse and orgasm, but not as a pass—fail test. If Brenda could embrace flexible orgasm as first class, Gary could embrace GES for himself and their relationship. Gary did not enjoy rubbing sex, but did value receiving manual and oral stimulation to orgasm. Brenda enjoyed his ejaculating in her mouth, but preferred to spit rather than swallow the semen. This was the clearest and most personal sexual discussion they'd ever had.

Sexuality with aging requires using all your psychological, bio-medical, and social-relational resources to promote desire/pleasure/eroticism/satisfaction. The critical issue for Brenda was to reassert her sexual voice, including her orgasmic voice. The critical issue for Gary was to affirm pleasure as more important than performance and to embrace GES rather than demand perfect intercourse.

Learning new information about sexual response with aging is empowering, but even more important is enacting new skills from the aging psychosexual skill exercises, accepting your aging body, and enjoying variable, flexible sexual expression. GES is so much easier for the man to accept if his partner affirms this approach. Brenda and Gary agreed that if sex did not flow to intercourse, they would transition to a mutual, synchronous erotic scenario.

In reintroducing intercourse, Brenda agreed to guide intromission. This allowed Gary to focus on multiple stimulation and not be distracted by fears concerning penile rigidity. Brenda's sexuality was enhanced by realizing Gary needed her and that he piggy-backed his arousal on hers.

Now in their mid-seventies, Brenda and Gary feel privileged to share a vital, satisfying couple sexuality. Their sexual relationship is quite different than Gary had imagined, but he felt proud they'd "beaten the odds". If there were two or three unsuccessful intercourse experiences, Gary would take a Viagra to boost vascular function and confidence, but most of the time he preferred to go with the flow and GES. He enjoyed being stimulated to orgasm orally, which was successful 95% of the time. Gary and Brenda accepted occasional erection problems as they did occasional desire or orgasm problems. Sexuality occurred weekly and was satisfying whether it involved intercourse and orgasm or not.

## The Importance of Implementing Psychosexual Skill Exercises

We are strong proponents of "knowledge is power". Acknowledge the advantages and challenges of sexuality with aging. Real and sustainable change comes with enacting the psychosexual skill exercises. Implementing these exercises makes the advantages of sexuality and aging personal and concrete, especially the role of relaxation, pleasuring, and giving yourself and your partner the time to build sexual responsivity. The challenges of sexuality and aging include using all your skills as intimate and erotic friends, embracing GES, when sex is dissatisfying or dysfunctional turning toward each other, valuing synchronous and asynchronous experiences, and confidently transitioning to sensual or erotic scenarios when sex does not flow to intercourse. The exercises allow you to create your unique couple sexual style which integrates intimacy and eroticism. It allows you to build "her", "his", and "our" bridges to sexual desire. Realizing you are not clones of each other adds spice to your sexual relationship.

## Three Psychosexual Skill Exercises

Rather than starting with non-genital touching and a prohibition on intercourse, begin with a trust position where you feel comfortable and securely attached. Be open to sensual, playful, and erotic touch. Each partner has the power to veto at least one and up to three sexual scenarios/techniques. You have the power to say "no" to a sexual scenario which is uncomfortable or negative. Be confident that your partner will honor your veto. Unless you have the power to say "no" you don't have the freedom to enjoy touching, pleasuring, and sexuality.

Take advantage of this freedom and create your preferred sexual scenario. How do you want to start, engage in pleasuring, and transition to eroticism, and what is your preferred intercourse position and type of thrusting? Do you enjoy multiple stimulation during intercourse?

What is your favorite afterplay scenario? Your scenario is usually different than your partner's. It is not a matter of right or wrong, but what fits you. Your scenario might be one you've enjoyed many times or something new. What fits you as an aging couple? It's probably quite different than sex in your 20s or 40s. Use this exercise to take advantage of the special dimensions of sexuality and aging.

For the second psychosexual skill exercise, focus on the roles of intercourse and erotic sexuality. Most males (and couples) believe that "sex=intercourse". Males especially fear erectile dysfunction (ED). The man believes any intercourse failure means he has ED. In fact, almost all men over 60 experience occasional erectile problems. Whether once a month, once every ten times, or once a year, at some point every man over 60 will not have an erection sufficient for intercourse. The GES model emphasizes the realistic expectation that 85% of sexual encounters will flow from relaxation to pleasure to arousal to erotic flow to intercourse. When sex does not flow, the couple seamlessly transition to an erotic or sensual scenario. No panicking and no apologizing. The key concept is that intercourse is a couple experience of sharing pleasure and eroticism, not an individual pass—fail test.

To make this personal and concrete we encourage you to experiment with proceeding to intercourse or choosing a mutual or asynchronous erotic experience. The key is the pleasure focus. Do not allow sex to be subverted by anticipatory or performance anxiety. For both the woman and man subjective arousal (feeling receptive, responsive, and "turned-on") is more important than objective arousal (erection and vaginal lubrication). The key is not to transition to intercourse until subjective arousal is at least a "7" and ideally "8". Typically, she uses a vaginal lubricant as part of the pleasuring/eroticism process.

The point of intromission can be a vulnerable time for both partners. To reduce anxiety and self-consciousness stay actively involved in giving and receiving pleasuring and erotic touch. Many couples find that the woman guiding intromission is a good strategy because she is the expert on her vagina and it allows the man to stay actively involved in the pleasuring/eroticism process rather than be distracted by erectile anxiety. You don't need a rigid penis to enjoy sensations inside the vagina. Intercourse, like other aspects of couple sexuality, is variable and flexible with aging.

Multiple stimulation during intercourse enhances pleasure and satisfaction. Giving and receiving stimulation increases eroticism. Both the woman and man have the freedom to use private erotic fantasies as a bridge to erotic flow and orgasm.

Using the GES approach, 85% of sexual encounters will flow to intercourse. When sexuality does not flow, rather than apologize or panic, comfortably transition to a sensual or erotic scenario. You are being sexual in a sensual or erotic manner. Try the alternative scenarios two to three times to be sure they are a good fit for you. Try a mutual, synchronous and an asynchronous erotic scenario at least twice. Which do you prefer?

The third exercise focuses on orgasm and satisfaction. For young couples, orgasm and satisfaction are used interchangeably, although that is not scientifically true. With couples over 60, it is crucial to explore the distinct roles of orgasm and satisfaction and to affirm the importance of both. Orgasm is a physiological response of heightened arousal/erotic flow resulting in your body "letting go" and experiencing rhythmic contractions and extreme pleasure for three to ten seconds. Satisfaction involves feeling good about yourself as a sexual person and energized as a sexual couple. Satisfaction certainly involves orgasm, but satisfaction is more than orgasm and is more important.

The man accepts a lessened need to ejaculate at each encounter. Most men are not aware of normal changes in orgasm and ejaculation with aging. Women are accustomed to variability in their orgasmic pattern—few women are orgasmic 100% of the time during couple sex. On average 70% of couple encounters involve female orgasm with the range of 30–90% (Graham, 2014). If sex were just about orgasm, both women and men would masturbate, a more reliable way to reach orgasm. By its nature, especially with aging, couple sexuality is variable and flexible.

Orgasm is integral to male and female sexuality. You learn to accept and enjoy non-orgasmic experiences and not feel this is a failure.

This exercise is best done a day after the man ejaculates and feels little or no ejaculatory demand. Engage in sensual, playful, erotic, and intercourse touch. Both partners can enjoy prolonged pleasuring and arousal as well as intercourse, but without the demand to ejaculate. If she is aroused and desires orgasm, you can enjoy her response, whether during intercourse or with manual, oral, or rubbing stimulation.

Make this a pleasurable, satisfying experience for both partners. You could cease intercourse and enjoy pleasuring, roll over and hold each other, ask for a whole-body massage, or sit, touch, and talk. You don't need an orgasm/ejaculation to feel sexually satisfied.

The trap for the man is to feel the experience is worthless if he doesn't ejaculate—and push himself to ejaculate. He is working against his body. She can have a satisfying experience without orgasm and so can he.

Ejaculation occurs when there is a desire for orgasm. Accept that it is normal to not ejaculate every time. This awareness enhances sexual satisfaction in your 60s, 70s, and 80s. An advantage of the aging process is it facilitates being an equitable sexual team who need each other to share pleasure and eroticism. Especially important is to recognize a sexual experience when one partner is orgasmic and the other isn't, but the non-orgasmic partner finds sex more satisfying. The woman finds it easier to accept GES and orgasmic variability because it is congruent with her lived sexual experiences. It is a challenge for the man, but the wise man embraces orgasmic variability and accepts the "new normal" rather than fight against his sexual body. The key to satisfaction is feeling good about yourself as a sexual person and bonded as a sexual couple.

## Summary

The 60s, 70s, and 80s are some of the best times to enjoy sensual, playful, and erotic sexuality. Experience intercourse as a couple process and celebrate variable, flexible couple sexuality. Satisfaction increases for couples who beat the odds and celebrate pleasure-oriented sexuality. You can enjoy your body, your partner's body, and couple sexuality. You need each other as intimate and erotic allies in a way you had not before. The multiple roles, meanings, and outcomes of sexuality are clearer with aging. The integration of intimacy, non-demand pleasuring, and eroticism reaches fruition with your aging.

# 13

# SEXUALLY, ONE SIZE NEVER FITS ALL

A core concept in the sexuality field is to honor diversity and individual differences. "Sexually, one size never fits all". It is crucial to accept your "authentic sexual self". So many people, both male and female, have a "contingent sexual self-esteem". You fear that if your partner knew things about you psychologically, relationally, or sexually they would not love or accept you. "Shameful sexual secrets" are a poison for the person and relationship (Epstein & Falconier, 2017).

We have emphasized traditional relationships in this book. Traditional means prioritizing your relationship (secure bond) with commitment to emotional and sexual monogamy. This includes not just married couples, but also partnered couples, lesbian couples, and a significant number of gay male couples. The important factor is that the emotional, relational, and sexual commitment is genuine. A "trap" for a traditional relationship is feeling hurt and betrayed by a partner's hidden sexual life and values. A frequent problem is extra-marital affairs (EMAs). Another frequent problem is that the sexual relationship is mediocre or dysfunctional rather than vital and satisfying.

There are many types of non-traditional sexual relationships. Non-traditional means different, not better or worse. This is not a conflict over "right—wrong" sexual values. That's self-defeating and pejorative toward other people's values. As long as the sexual experience is not forced or coerced, does not involve children under 16, is done in private, and is not compulsive or self-destructive, the sexual relationship is in the normal range. The issue is expressing your authentic sexual self so that sexuality has a positive 15–20% role in your life and relationship.

The most common form of non-traditional sexuality is a rejection of monogamy. This does not mean having a secret sexual life of affairs, paid sex, online sex, or random sex. Instead, the couple develop a consensual non-monogamy agreement. We examine this issue in Chapter 14 (Monogamy vs. Consensual Non-Monogamy). This is a very personal, value-oriented issue. Be clear whether you adhere to traditional or non-traditional sexual values. Either way, you deserve for sexuality to have a positive role in your life and relationship.

Honoring individual, couple, cultural, and value differences is crucial. Leading a secret sexual life or pretending one thing and living something totally different is hard on the person, relationship, and couple sexuality. The best measure of psychological and sexual well-being is that your attitudes, behaviors, and emotions are congruent.

An example of sexual incongruence was a gay man who married a woman and had children to prove he was "normal" and for social acceptance. Living a lie was unhealthy for the man, woman, and family. Sexual orientation for gay men is "hard-wired". It is not changed by marriage or fatherhood. Congruence is served by accepting that his authentic sexual self is gay. The challenge is to psychologically, relationally, and sexually live his life in a healthy manner. The challenge is to be a healthy gay man who deserves sexuality to have a positive role in his life and relationship. Accepting being gay is optimal for him.

Your sexual attitudes, behavior, and feelings are accepted as normal whether traditional or non-traditional. For example, the gay man might have a "monogamish" agreement with his partner that each is free to have sex with other men as long as they practice safe sex and other sexual relationships do not subvert their bond. Some gay couples make a traditional monogamy commitment. The issue of traditional vs. non-traditional values is not a "right—wrong" issue, but what is the right fit for the person and their relationship. In accepting the "sexually, one size never fits all" concept, the issue is what is the best decision for you and your relationship, not what is "socially desirable". Accepting your authentic sexual self is the basis for a wise decision. Living with sexual secrets and basing your emotional choice on the approval of others or of societal standards causes pain and damage to self and others.

In the past, gay men were expected (even coerced) to marry with the mistaken belief that marriage would resolve sexual orientation conflicts. Instead, it resulted in the man having a secret sexual life, sometimes involving high-risk sex. This "resolution" was in no one's best interest—not the man, the spouse, the family, or the culture. Being gay was a "shameful secret" which was stigmatized and punished. We should never return to the "old days".

The challenge is to own your authentic sexual self and live life in a psychologically, relationally, and sexually healthy manner. Sadly, people make "emotional choices" rather than "wise decisions". Accepting your authentic sexual self is the foundation for a wise decision. Having sexual secrets and basing your emotional choices on the approval of others or society causes damage to self and others.

The guideline about authentic sexual self is true for both women and men. A common female trap is marrying because of an unplanned pregnancy and pressure from family. Rather than marriage based on a respectful, trusting, emotional commitment, it was based on the pregnancy. Although couples can and do create a genuine marital bond, sadly this often results in an alienated marriage, and eventually divorce. A psychological guideline is that positive motivation promotes wise decisions. Negative motivation (especially shame) subverts the person and relationship.

## Dealing with Negative Sexual Experiences

Confusing, negative, and traumatic sexual experiences are almost universal among women and men. The key is to deal with these so they do not control you and your sexuality. Primary prevention is optimal—there should not be abusive or negative sexual experiences. Secondary prevention means the experience is discussed and processed at the time rather than being secret. Rather than feeling shameful, process the sexual experience and understand that it is not the child's or adolescent's fault. The responsibility lies with the perpetrator, who should apologize. You accept the reality of the sexual experience, which includes discussing negative and positive learnings. Most important, your adult sexual self-esteem is that of a proud survivor, not an anxious, depressed, or angry victim.

Unfortunately, this is not what happens for the majority of people. They feel confused, anxious, or guilty and the abusive experience becomes controlling. Do not allow your sexual self-esteem to be controlled by a negative experience. The key to sexual self-esteem is accepting your strengths and vulnerabilities psychologically, relationally, and sexually. This promotes acceptance of your authentic sexual self. Acceptance is necessary, but not sufficient. The key is living your life as a healthy sexual person. This means expressing sexuality in a manner which enhances your life and relationship. Hopefully, others affirm and support your sexuality, but you are not dependent on the approval of others.

An example involves sexual orientation. As a culture, we have come a long way in the past 50 years. In the past, being gay was labeled a "perversion" or "deviation". In 2020 being gay is accepted as a normal sexual variation. We go further and believe that for a gay man, embracing being gay and living his life as a first-class gay man is healthy for him, his relationship, and the culture. This is equally true for lesbian women. Many well-intentioned (and some not well-intentioned) people do not accept that being lesbian or gay is healthy. The gay man or lesbian woman cannot be controlled by their judgment. Self-acceptance and the support of others outweighs cultural prejudices.

The challenge is to live your life in a healthy manner where sexuality has a positive role. This means valuing the 15–20% role of sexuality for you and your relationship as well as confronting negative sexual attitudes, behaviors, and emotions. We will explore three case examples to illustrate that sexually one size never fits all.

## Gloria

As a 37-year-old woman Gloria felt she had finally identified her authentic sexual self and was living her life as a healthy sexual woman. Gloria had married her high school boyfriend at 23. At age 32 she believed she had a "normal" life as a married woman with children ages 7, 4, and 2 and pursuing her career as a physical therapist. However, something did not fit for Gloria. She loved her husband and family, but she did not feel in love with him. She could orgasm, but did not feel desire, pleasure, or satisfaction.

Gloria felt emotionally connected to a divorced female friend and was aware of a growing physical attraction to her. Throughout her life Gloria had noticed emotional and physical feelings toward women, but had never acted on these feelings.

Her friend, Caroline, agreed to stay overnight when Gloria's husband was at a work meeting. Caroline brought her 7-year-old daughter, who was friendly with Gloria's 7-year-old son. After dinner, baths, and putting the children to sleep, Caroline and Gloria watched a Netflix movie. It was a romantic comedy that they really enjoyed, whilst laughing and engaging in silly touching. After the movie, the touching became more serious and pleasure-oriented. Gloria was aware of how receptive and responsive she felt with Caroline, more so than with her husband. Gloria felt turned-on by Caroline's responsivity, which included Caroline being orgasmic when Gloria kissed her and gave breast stimulation. Gloria was aware of feeling emotionally and physically turned on. Gloria recalled similar feelings from experiences in adolescence and young adulthood.

When she married, Gloria felt this part of her life was resolved. The birth of each child reinforced her commitment to the marriage and family. Gloria realized what she felt with Caroline was real, not just the excitement of an illicit experience. Gloria needed to make meaning of her experiences. She sought individual therapy as a resource to help her make a wise decision for herself and her family. With guidance from the therapist, Gloria carefully assessed her past and present attitudes, behavior, and emotions about sexuality and sexual orientation.

After five months of therapy, the individual therapist referred Gloria to a couple therapist who was empathic and respectful of both the husband and Gloria. The couple therapist was pro-relationship and pro-sexual, but not anti-divorce. She advocated for a "good divorce" rather than the usual "bad divorce", where the dominant emotion is anger with a cycle of blame—counter-blame. In the good divorce, Gloria and the ex-husband's shared emotion was sadness, they wished each other well, and focused on co-parenting. They agreed to stay out of the ex-spouse's psychological, relational, and sexual decisions. This was particularly important for Gloria, who focused on understanding and accepting herself. This included whether she was lesbian, bi-sexual, or fluid in her sexual orientation. The ex-husband accepted that differences in sexual orientation were the major factor in the divorce and that they would be respectful, cooperative co-parents. Gloria was committed to make a wise decision about her sexuality. She did not want his input, nor did she need his approval. Gloria wanted sexuality to have a positive role in her life. She was discovering her authentic sexual self.

## Rex and Andrea

Sex had not been a strength of Rex and Andrea's four-year marriage. However, they saw themselves as a satisfied, secure couple who were very excited to have their first baby in four months. Andrea valued being an affectionate couple, but in the fifth month of pregnancy sex was not high on her agenda. She wondered what was happening with Rex sexually. He joked he was taking care of himself. Andrea had powerful memories of their eight-month romantic love/passionate sex (limerance) phase before marriage. She was confused about how sex had become bland and infrequent. She felt good about sex during the high probability week and the ensuing pregnancy.

Andrea wondered about the packages coming to Rex from on-line purchases. Although she knew it was wrong, she opened a package and was shocked to discover it was full of enhanced bra materials. When she asked Rex, he was at first very embarrassed and then very angry, accusing her of being a "sex detective". Rex said this was none of her business. Unfortunately, Gloria and Rex fell into an attack—counterattack power struggle, featuring name-calling and accusations.

Approximately 4% of men have an atypical (variant or kinky) arousal pattern. The most common is a fetish, next crossdressing, and then BDSM. Variant arousal is in the normal range of sexuality and is totally different than deviant arousal, which is harmful to others and illegal (the most common type is exhibitionism).

Rex had a variant arousal (fetish) to breast enhancement materials. This had developed in adolescence and increasingly controlled his sexual response, both with masturbation and couple sex. Andrea was surprised, as well as relieved, to learn that the variant arousal pattern existed before she met Rex. She did not cause this fetish.

Rex had never disclosed his atypical sexual arousal to a woman, although he wrote about it on three breast material fetish sites and felt his atypical arousal pattern was accepted. People on the site urged him to enjoy the fetish. At least one of those sites benefitted financially from his purchases. Andrea made the point that she could have purchased the breast enhancement material for much less money.

Rex had always been secretive about sexuality. The "poison" was the combination of high secrecy, high eroticism, and high shame. Andrea realized this was not healthy for Rex, her, or their relationship. Rex felt self-conscious speaking about the fetish, but realized it was important to do so. Fetishes are a normal variant of sexual arousal. The issue is whether to accept the fetish and include it in couple sexuality, compartmentalize the fetish, or accept a "necessary loss" strategy and give up the fetish. It is not a "right—wrong" choice, but a decision about what is the right fit for that man and couple. This decision is usually made with the help of a couple sex therapist (suggestions for finding a therapist are in Appendix A).

Rex wanted to use the compartmentalization strategy. Traditionally, this had been the most commonly employed strategy. The fetish was used during masturbation and as a fantasy during couple sex to ensure he could function sexually. The woman had no role. For most couples, this is the least sexually satisfying strategy. The typical result is that couple sex is infrequent and unsatisfying for the man (and woman). Andrea felt left out and devalued sexually. Rex had a split sexual life where masturbation with the fetish material was highly erotic, but couple sex a chore.

The newest strategy is sexual acceptance. The man accepts that fetish arousal is key to his erotic response. The woman is accepting rather than judgmental. She is a sexual friend who is open to incorporating his "kink" into their couple sexual style. Rather than feeling sexually inadequate or rejected, she accepts the fetish as an erotic turn-on for him. The role of erotic materials or fantasies is as a bridge to desire and a bridge to erotic flow and orgasm. The challenge for Andrea and Rex was to see if they could incorporate the fetish material into couple sexuality.

The third strategy, necessary loss, is what most women advocate and the man resists. If the strategy is motivated by shame, it almost always fails. Rather than a bridge that joins the couple, the fetish is a sexual wall which isolates the man and cannot be integrated into couple sexuality. This occurs when the woman finds the fetish anti-erotic, or the man finds that when he enacts the fetish with his partner it loses its erotic charge. With necessary loss, the challenge is to find a new couple sexual style which integrates eroticism. The erotic charge is less intense for the man, but he can enjoy couple sexuality without a secret sexual life.

The issue of variant/atypical sexual arousal is a poignant example that sexually one size never fits all. The ideal scenario is acceptance which enhances erotic response for both partners. A positive trend, rather than a sexual secret, is to encourage the man to discuss variant arousal/fetish within 6 months of meeting a partner so she has the choice of accepting it or ending the relationship (hopefully, on good terms). Another trend is people who meet via a "kink-friendly" website and explore a potential relationship.

Some men find that the atypical/variant arousal works best as an erotic fantasy. When he plays it out he becomes self-conscious and it's an erotic dud. Other couples find the variant arousal (whether involving cross-dressing, a BDSM scenario, "talking dirty", watching a porn video, playing out an erotic fantasy, or being sexual outdoors or in front of a mirror) is a special erotic treat, to use on occasion, but not on a regular basis. The key is what fits for both partners and your relationship.

## Risa and Taylor

A third example involves Risa and Taylor, who were a couple for seven years. Each had been divorced (Risa twice and Taylor once). They valued an emotional/sexual partnership, but not marriage. They valued non-traditional sexuality in its many dimensions. Taylor was a principal in an economics consulting practice and traveled for business both nationally and internationally. Risa was a mental health counselor who worked in a community agency and had her own practice. They had a consensual non-monogamy agreement (CNM) which added variety and spice to their sexual life. Taylor was a rational, high-powered, in-control consultant. However, sexually he preferred the submissive role. Risa enjoyed being sexually selfish, and the extent to which Taylor was turned-on by her sexual intensity and assuming sexual control. Couple sexuality involved his "servicing" her sexual demands with her being multi-orgasmic. They thought of themselves as a sexually free, liberated, open couple.

The sexual secret was that when he worked internationally, Taylor engaged in voyeurism (he was a "peeping tom"). This is a deviant behavior because even though his victims were adults they did not consent to being sexually observed. Voyeurism is an illegal activity. He'd only been caught twice by police and both times paid a bribe so he was not prosecuted. However, the third time he was arrested and sentenced to three years probation in a country he had to return to because of consulting contracts. Taylor convinced his firm that this was just a drunken mistake. When Risa discovered the arrest, she realized this was a severe problem.

The power struggle so many couples fall into is the woman demanding the man change the problematic sexual behavior, and the man minimizing and avoiding. A healthy approach is the man takes responsibility for the sex problem and asks his partner to be an emotional and sexual ally in the change process. Risa being angry at Taylor and shaming him made a difficult situation worse. Taylor's denial and avoidance fueled the negative cycle.

Dealing with deviant sexuality usually requires professional intervention with a sexual specialist. In an empathic, respectful, yet confrontative manner, the therapist was clear that voyeurism was a deviant behavior, harmful to the unwitting victim. The therapist affirmed Risa and Taylor's CNM, but questioned Taylor's sexual role with Risa and other partners. Although Taylor was orgasmic during couple sex, the experience was much less involving than the voyeurism and masturbation. These were new insights for Risa who had believed Taylor was a very pro-sexual man. In fact, Taylor viewed couple sex as for the woman, not for him. He enjoyed sex with Risa and valued her erotic response, but held himself back. For Taylor voyeurism was a 10 on a 10-point scale of subjective arousal while partner sex was 4–5. Taylor had convinced himself that voyeurism was a "victimless" event. He had to use all his resources, including honesty with Risa, to eliminate voyeuristic activities and fantasies.

An important strategy was for Taylor to increase desire/pleasure/eroticism/satisfaction in couple sexuality, with Risa and other partners. Couple sex wasn't just to service the woman and revel in her sexual response. Taylor learned to be an active, involved partner and embrace couple sexuality.

## What It Means to be Your Authentic Sexual Self

A key to healthy sexuality is self-acceptance. Express your sexuality so that it has a genuine 15–20% role in your life and relationship. This is true for both traditional and non-traditional sexuality. The issue is not "right", "better", or "perfect". The issue is what is sexually healthy for you.

In many ways, traditional sexuality is easier to understand and express—the parameters are clear and you receive social support. The challenge for non-traditional sexuality is to ensure it is genuine. You need to do more than reject traditional sexuality. You must ensure that psychologically, relationally, and sexually your sexual expression is authentic and healthy for you and your relationship.

Choose a partner and relationship where non-traditional sexuality will have a positive role for both partners and energize your relationship. In addition, you need to agree on boundary issues. What behaviors subvert you and your relationship. It is valuable to have friends and/or a support group who affirm your sexual feelings and preferences. You are not dependent on their approval, but benefit from their support of your non-traditional sexuality.

### Exercise: Identifying and Implementing Your Authentic Sexual Self

This exercise involves two phases. First, in an affirmative manner be clear about your attitudes, behavior, and emotions which promote sexual health. Be honest with yourself and your partner (or potential partner). The best measure of sexual well-being is when your attitudes, behavior, and emotions are positive and congruent.

The key question is whether your sexual values are traditional, non-traditional, or a mixture. For example, many people are traditional in prioritizing their relationship and a commitment to monogamy, but have a sexual preference they are embarrassed to share with their partner. This exercise challenges you to break this pattern and establish a genuine dialogue about the role of sexuality in your life and relationship. You can't expect your partner to be supportive if you are not honest with them.

This allows you to dialogue about what sexual components can be integrated, what components can be modified, and which components will not fit. You owe it to yourself and your relationship to disclose your authentic sexual self whether traditional, non-traditional, or mixed. Awareness and self-acceptance are the base from which to dialogue with your partner.

An example is the woman who is committed to her marriage, monogamy, and intercourse. She has never told her partner that her preferred erotic/orgasmic pattern is with manual stimulation—she fakes orgasm during intercourse. Disclosing this sensitive material is healthy for her and your relationship. Rather than feeling embarrassed or guilty about the past, accept that you can learn from the past but cannot change the past. Your power for change is in the present. Disclose and process sexual issues, feelings, and preferences.

A non-traditional example is the man who blames his partner's weight for their low sex frequency. The truth is he much prefers masturbation to couple sex. He has a sense of self-efficacy with masturbation, but has always been highly anxious during couple sex. He chose this partner because she was overweight so he could blame her for the sex problem. Can he be honest with himself and her in requesting to use self-stimulation during partner sex so that couple sexuality has a positive role in their lives?

A mixed example is a couple with a functional sexual relationship, but one which is neither special nor energizing. The issue for the man is he has a powerful desire to receive oral stimulation to orgasm and for his wife to swallow the semen. However, he is too shy to request this, so each sexual encounter ends with intercourse. He enjoys intercourse and ejaculating in her vagina, but the routine of this scenario subverts its erotic charge. He is so worried she will reject his oral sex scenario or misinterpret it as sexually degrading that he avoids raising the topic. They take turns giving and receiving oral sex as part of pleasuring/eroticism. Her assumption is that oral sexuality is a strength of their sexual relationship. She is surprised and hurt when he finally discloses his preferred scenario, but is glad he did.

The second phase of this exercise is a couple dialogue focused on deciding whether this request can be integrated into your sexual relationship, modified, or won't work for one or both partners. Open communication is necessary, but not sufficient. Implementation is the vital factor.

The best sex is mutual and synchronous, which means both partners experience desire/pleasure/eroticism/satisfaction. Yet, most sexual encounters are asynchronous, i.e. better for one partner than the other. Asynchronous sexuality is not only normal, it is healthy and adds spice and variety to couple sexuality. However, there is a caveat. Asynchronous sex cannot be at the expense of the partner or your relationship. To be specific, if the requesting person feels this sexual scenario would result in a 10 on subjective arousal for him, but is a −5 for the partner, it is not acceptable. More commonly the scenario is a 10 for the requesting partner and a 3 or 4 for the other. This is accepted and played out. The key is finding genuine common ground so sexuality has a positive role for your relationship. By its nature, an asynchronous sexual scenario is better for the requesting partner than the other. To return to the example, being fellated to orgasm and the partner swallowing the semen is a stronger erotic charge for the man than the woman. As long as it's not negative for her, integrating this scenario into your couple sexuality is good. If swallowing semen is aversive, she can spit the semen into a Kleenex. Couple sexuality is based on a positive influence process, not on sexual demands at the expense of the partner.

Sexuality is not just about attitudes, feelings, and communication, it involves real-life sexual enactment. The question is whether a new scenario is pleasurable and erotic or whether it is better in fantasy than in real life. A core understanding is that erotic fantasy is very different than real-life sexual behavior. In this exercise, both communication and sexual expression need to be positive. This ensures the sexual scenario is erotic and satisfying.

### When One Partner's Authentic Sexual Self is in Conflict with the Other's Sexuality

The ideal scenario is each partner is their authentic sexual self which enhances couple sexuality. The couple value both mutual, synchronous scenarios and asynchronous sexual experiences. However, often one person's preferred sexual scenario and technique does not fit for the partner or their relationship. Sometimes sexual conflicts reflect a "fatally flawed sexual relationship". Others stop being sexual, but remain a couple and family. More commonly, the couple agree to a "good divorce" because of core sexual differences. An example is where the spouse discloses that she is lesbian and this difference in sexual orientation causes one or both to decide this is a fatally flawed marriage.

When the person's authentic sexual self is unable to be integrated into couple sexuality it is not a matter of "good—bad" where the emotion is anger with the struggle of who is wrong. A healthy approach is to recognize this difference as a fatal flaw in the relationship. The emotion is sadness rather than anger. As you dissolve your partnership (marriage), wish each other well as you transition to the next chapter of your life. Sadly, many people remain angry for years after the break-up. Their lives remain burdened by struggles over sex and whose fault it was that the relationship ended. Sexual self-esteem is controlled by past conflicts. A very unwise choice. The wise decision is to accept the sexual differences, learn from the past, and make wise decisions in the present and future.

## Summary

The core of healthy sexuality is accepting your authentic sexual self. Be sure your sexual attitudes, behavior, and feelings are congruent. Dialogue with your partner about what fits and what does not fit in your sexual relationship. Be clear about your sexual values—are they traditional or non-traditional? What do you need for sexuality to have a healthy 15–20% role for both individuals and your relationship? Be genuine and authentic, don't give the socially desirable answer. Don't let other peoples' sexual values (including the authors of this book) take precedence over your sexual values, feelings, and behavior. Sexually one size does not fit all. Find the right sexual fit for you and your relationship.

# 14

# MONOGAMY VS. CONSENSUAL NON-MONOGAMY

The traditional assumption was that married couples (in fact all couples) adhered to emotional and sexual monogamy. In the strict understanding, this meant no fantasy or emotional attraction to anyone else. Certainly, no touching or sexual activity, especially not intercourse.

Jealousy, fears, and suspicions about affairs (EMAs) dominate songs, movies, novels, TV dramas. The condemnation of EMAs was almost universal. A striking reality is that very few couples had an explicit, personal discussion about the EMA issue.

EMAs have existed throughout history and across cultures, especially male EMAs. This was based on the traditional male—female double standard that men value sex, have higher desire, and "a real man never says no to sex". In the double standard, the woman values intimacy, affection, and relational security. The fear was that a pro-sexual woman would be prone to EMAs. The rules of the double standard were clear, but harmful to women, men, couples, and the culture. Typically, a female EMA was strongly condemned and punished (sometimes to death) while a male EMA was accepted as "normal male behavior" as long as it didn't disrupt the family.

Like any sexual behavior, EMAs are multi-causal, multi-dimensional, with large individual, couple, cultural, and value differences. The issue of EMAs has achieved prominence with the introduction of a new concept—consensual non-monogamy (CNM) (Perel, 2017). CNM encourages couples (whether married, partnered, lesbian, or gay) to develop a specific agreement about emotional and sexual experiences with others.

Rather than assuming monogamy as the only acceptable way to be in a relationship, CNM challenges this assumption. A crucial sexual concept is that "one size never fits all". Traditional couples affirm the value of monogamy. Traditional means more than heterosexual married couples. The majority of partnered and lesbian couples affirm a monogamy agreement, as do a significant number of gay male couples. Rather than being governed by tradition, social norms, or the "socially desirable" response, you are urged to make a personally relevant emotional commitment to monogamy (rather than assuming monogamy). If you have non-traditional values, you need to develop a specific agreement about CNM. Secret EMAs are destructive to your relationship.

**Values**

Sex and relationships are about values. When people (including therapists and writers) say they are value-free they are lying to you and to themselves. In terms of monogamy vs. CNM, it is not a question of "right—wrong". It is a question of what is the right fit for you as a person and a couple. Power struggles between traditional and non-traditional couples about who is "wrong" is not in the best interest of the sexuality field nor in your best interest. This is especially true of monogamy and CNM issues. Labeling traditional couples as "rigid and fearful" or non-traditional couples as "social deviates" or "immoral" is unfair. The healthy approach is deciding what is the right fit attitudinally, behaviorally, and emotionally for you and your relationship. We urge you to make "wise decisions", not "emotional choices". Wise means it makes sense emotionally and practically and is healthy in the short and long term.

Clandestine EMAs were typically driven by impulse and emotion and often had disastrous outcomes for the person and relationship. The drama of the EMA was driven by secrecy and breaking boundaries. What made for a great EMA was very different than a satisfying, secure, and sexual relationship. EMA sex is almost always better than marital sex. EMA sex is like the limerance phase multiplied by three with its secrecy, illicitness, and broken boundaries. We are opposed to clandestine EMAs because of their impact on you and your relationship. Secrecy causes feelings of betrayal, which impact the person, the partner, and their relationship.

The issue of monogamy vs. CNM is a different issue. It asks you and your partner to be honest in terms of your authentic sexual self and the meaning of your relationship. Those who decide on monogamy typically place high value on intimacy and security. Those who decide on CNM value autonomy, eroticism, and exploring boundaries. Each choice has potential vulnerabilities and challenges. You can't have it all. You owe it to yourself, your partner, your relationship, and your family to make a wise decision.

## Vulnerabilities and Challenges of Monogamy

The biggest vulnerability for traditional couples is to treat monogamy as a default position rather than a genuine commitment. The couple take a "holier than thou" stance and stigmatize non-traditional couples. When the monogamy agreement is violated (which occurs for 35–45% of married couples, with higher rates for partnered and cohabitating couples) it causes major disruptions for both the involved and injured partners (Allen et al., 2005). The injured partner often reacts in a PTSD (post-traumatic stress disorder) manner. The relationship becomes defined by the EMA, even years later. Many couples never rebuild their trust bond or their sexual relationship. Sexuality is controlled by the EMA legacy.

People say with all the problems of non-monogamy, why would anyone choose CNM? Remember a core adage: "Sexually, one size never fits all". Some individuals and couples feel that monogamy stifles them and subverts sexual desire. Rather than judging or putting down non-traditional couples, traditional couples would be better to put time and energy into ensuring that their monogamy agreement is clear and strong, especially valuing the 15–20% role of sex in their relationship.

In dealing with potential vulnerabilities, the first step is to be sure your monogamy agreement is personally relevant, positively motivated, and shared with your spouse (life partner). That does not mean a five-minute conversation. It involves a series of dialogues about your authentic self (especially your sexual self) where you explore genuine strengths and vulnerabilities. It involves an exploration of your relationship models (your family, dating relationships, whether you value a satisfying, secure, and sexual relationship). It means exploring what facilitates desire/pleasure/eroticism/satisfaction in your relationship. Monogamy is not about easy words or good intentions. Monogamy requires awareness and commitment. For you, how important is an intimate sexual relationship and how valuable is monogamy? Do you put a priority on your relationship and monogamy? Don't give a "socially desirable" answer. Give clear, personally relevant answers.

We will explore this in detail in the exercise section, but be aware of what would make you vulnerable to an EMA. We believe all individuals and all relationships have vulnerabilities. What type of situation, person, or emotion would make you vulnerable? A powerful insight is that few partners share the same vulnerabilities. For example, one person might feel vulnerable when depressed or lonely while the partner is vulnerable when celebrating a success surrounded by admiring people.

Vulnerabilities do not mean you are a bad person or have a troubled relationship. Vulnerabilities are part of being a human being. People used to believe that the major cause of an EMA was an unhappy marriage. The science says that the majority of EMAs occur in happy marriages (Allen et al., 2005). Another common misbelief is that sexual problems are a major cause of EMAs—again, science found this to be a myth. The reality is that EMAs are multi-causal, multi-dimensional, with large individual, relational, cultural, and value differences (Baucom et al., 2017).

An important understanding is that usually the injured partner misunderstands the involved partner's motivations for the EMA. Traditionally, males are more likely to have an EMA. In that case the woman is the injured partner. She treats the EMA as if it were the type of EMA she would have rather than the EMA he had. These misunderstandings are reinforced by gender stereotypes, media myths, and friends and relatives.

The most common male EMA is "high opportunity—low involvement". Whether a paid sexual experience, on-line sex, or "hook-up" sex, the man typically discounts the importance by saying this is normal male sex behavior, having nothing to do with the spouse or relationship. Usually, high opportunity—low involvement is the easiest EMA to deal with.

The most challenging EMA is a female "comparison" affair where more of the emotional and sexual needs are met in the EMA than the marriage. Partly because of the mix of emotional and sexual dimensions and partly because it's a reversal of the double standard, the comparison EMA is most difficult for the couple to deal with. The man's sense of emotional and sexual betrayal compounds the impact.

A significant majority of couples (as many as 80–85%) commit to monogamy after an EMA. Almost no professionals and few couples support secret EMAs. Develop a genuine emotional and sexual agreement that affirms monogamy.

Be aware of the types and causes of EMA. These include high opportunity, boredom, finding a lost part of yourself, a symptom of depression or bi-polar disorder, peer pressure, to get back at the spouse, to see if you are sexually functional with another person or in another situation, a reason to end a fatally flawed marriage, acting out a secret arousal pattern, part of an alcohol or drug abuse culture, or EMA as a social or political statement. The relevant question is what would make you vulnerable to an EMA? What would make your spouse vulnerable? Don't assume and don't pretend. Dialogue with your partner about personal and relational vulnerabilities.

People don't believe the science. Scientifically, the most common cause for EMA is high opportunity (Glass, 2003). For example, certain professions are high opportunity for EMA—road warriors (blue collar or white collar), athletes and entertainers, police officers, bartenders. Women who work outside the home have more EMAs than homemakers—again, the opportunity factor. High opportunity EMAs tend to be impulsive, emotional, and short term (although there are important exceptions). If one or both partners in a traditional relationship are in a high opportunity situation, it is crucial that you have a clear, specific agreement to reinforce the value of monogamy.

Good intentions are necessary, but not sufficient. Dialogue about the value of monogamy, personal and relational vulnerabilities, and specific strategies and techniques to deal with risks. Enhance awareness and value monogamy for positive emotional and sexual reasons. Monogamy should not be based on fear, jealousy, or hyper vigilance. Fear motivation is unhealthy for you and your relationship. Positive motivation reinforces personal, relational, and sexual health. A core value of a monogamous relationship is to reinforce intimacy and security.

## Non-Traditional Values: Consensual Non-Monogamy (CNM)

Non-traditional couples advocate for CNM to enhance sexual autonomy, vitality, eroticism, and welcome diverse emotional and sexual experiences. They believe that CNM is healthier for all concerned. Consensual EMAs promote limerance feelings—it allows you to feel alive and experience sex and relationships in a new way.

The key is clarity about what you value in your primary relationship and what you want from your CNM relationship(s). For example, is the CNM meant to be a six-month passionate sex/dramatic experience, do you want a romantic week away, or are you part of a polyamorous community? Be clear with yourself, your partner, and your CNM partner(s). Focus on the positive motivation before discussing potential problems or traps. Don't treat the CNM like a perfect holiday movie, but as a personally meaningful life adventure. For example, the "road warrior" who had gone to bars hoping to meet a woman for a night, but feared discovery or a terrible experience, now tells his wife that when traveling he will meet a sexual friend. The woman will use contraception and he a condom. He will only be sexual when away from home for three nights or longer. His wife acknowledges this and tells him that is not the type of CNM relationship she wants. Her agreement was to have a sexual friend (who the husband did not know). She would see him away from their home and when the husband was not available. She assured her husband that pregnancy and HIV/STI would not be a risk. Although it was a serious, ongoing CNM, she would not engage in kissing with her sexual friend.

A different example of CNM was a couple who became involved in a swinging community. They would only be involved with other couples and would not be present when the spouse was sexual with another partner.

The number of potential variations and agreements for CNM is large. The issue is what each partner wants from CNM. For some it is the excitement of exploring a new relationship, for others the key is an unpredictable sexual adventure, and for still others it is being accepted in an alternative sexuality community. For CNM to be successfully adopted there needs to be a positive agenda, not just a rejection of traditional sexual values.

CNM does not need the approval of society or religion. CNM is promoted by acceptance from the partner and support of others. The strongest argument for CNM is it reflects the person's authentic sexual self.

### The Crucial Importance of Positive Motivation

In making an individual and couple decision, it is crucial that it be positively motivated, not a reaction to negative experiences, fears, or social judgment.

Those who decide on CNM need to be clear, individually and as a couple, about the psychological, relational, and sexual benefits they hope for. Those who decide on monogamy need to be clear about the benefits of their monogamy commitment. It is a very important life decision—you cannot have it all. Couples who decide on CNM need to address issues of emotional intimacy and relational stability. Couples who decide on monogamy need to ensure that their sexual relationship remains vital and satisfying. Monogamous couples recognize you give up unpredictability, adventure, and drama. CNM couples risk personal and relational disruption. Again, the issue is what is the right fit for you.

---

## Callie and Derek

Callie and Derek had been a couple for four years when they married last year—Callie was 36 and Derek 34. They prided themselves in being socially and politically progressive. They decided not to have children so Callie had a tubal ligation before the marriage. Both Callie and Derek were proud to be pro-sexual with a variety of partners and experiences.

It was Callie who brought up the issue of CNM. She assured Derek that she valued him and the stability of their relationship. She valued sexuality and felt it would be more exciting and satisfying if open to sex with others. Derek and his male friends joked about "open relationships", but the assumption was that it would be the man who was sexually open, not the woman. Derek was not a traditional double standard man, but did worry that Callie would find sex with another man more exciting. She teased him that no woman could be as sexually adventurous as she. They seriously dialogued about the sexual benefits of an open relationship as well as their concerns. They were surprised how similar they were about the pluses—feelings of desire and being desired, the drama of limerance sex, envy from their traditional couple friends, weekends away with a new partner, the drama of a roller coaster relationship. Callie valued being a "new woman". Derek liked the excitement of one-night stands.

What were different were each spouse's fears and vulnerabilities. Callie's fear was that Derek would be seduced by a manipulative woman with a financial agenda. Derek's fear was that sex would cause Callie to fall in love with the new partner and leave him. Derek's experience with family and friends was that it was always the woman who left the marriage.

In their dialogue, Callie made it clear that it would be intriguing and sexually exciting to hear about Derek's sexual partners, but she had no interest in meeting the woman or observing them being sexual. Derek had no interest in hearing about Callie's CNM, but wanted a clear red line about Callie falling in love with another man. He wanted CNM to add to their sexual lives, not interfere with couple sexuality or destabilize their relationship. The other red line for Derek is that Callie not be sexual with anyone he knew—friends, family, or neighbors. Derek realized this was unfair because the women he was most interested in were divorced friends of Callie's. Fair or not, these were Derek's boundaries.

They agreed if the CNM was causing distress or concerns, they would raise the issue within a week rather than let it fester. Also, every six months they would discuss how the CNM was going and if there were potential problems.

Derek and Callie did not judge their couple friends who had traditional values, but were convinced that CNM was right for them.

## Dylan and Rafael

Dylan and Rafael were viewed by family and friends as a very special couple. Each was the first in their family to graduate college. They were a committed couple. Unfortunately, they had never talked in a specific, personal way about sexuality or monogamy. Dylan's assumption was that sex was primarily Rafael's domain and they would be a monogamous couple so there was no need for a serious discussion. Rafael felt good about their sexual relationship and gave little thought to EMA issues. He assumed that a "real man" would never say no to a sexual opportunity. He felt a sexual dalliance would have no impact on Dylan or their relationship.

Sex and monogamy cannot be treated with benign neglect. Dylan heard that a male friend was having a secret EMA. When the wife discovered the EMA it set off a dramatic conflict which spread to their friend network. As often happens, couples split along gender roles. Dylan had great empathy for the wife and her feelings of betrayal. Rafael did not defend the EMA, but said the husband was a good guy and the wife was overreacting. The conversation between Rafael and Dylan generated much heat, but little light. This is a typical gender power struggle about the meaning of an EMA.

Dylan insisted that she and Rafael have a genuine dialogue about the role and meaning of sex and monogamy in their lives and marriage. At first, Rafael felt he was unfairly put on the defensive as a "bad guy". Dylan said her intention was to strengthen their marriage, not put down Rafael. Dylan shared stories of her parents' marriage and the marriages of other relatives and friends. The theme of these stories was that men could have high opportunity EMAs if it didn't threaten the marriage, but if the wife had an EMA "all hell broke loose" and she was labeled a "bad woman". Dylan said as college graduates and an aware couple they did not have to play out the old sexual script. She would not accept the double standard. She and Rafael had to create a genuine agreement that was applicable to both. Rafael misunderstood and felt that Dylan wanted to have an EMA. She said the opposite. She did not want an EMA, but if she were to have an EMA it would be a sexual friendship or a serious relationship. This was not acceptable to Rafael. He valued an intimate marriage with a spouse who was committed to him. Dylan affirmed that was her desire, but if Rafael wanted a dalliance EMA he could not dictate the type of EMA she could have. Just as important, Dylan did not want an EMA agreement based on fear or a "tit for tat" bargain. She wanted both to value monogamy because it promoted the intimacy and security of their bond. Rafael and Dylan shared responsibility for maintaining strong, resilient desire as part of their monogamy commitment. However, sexual problems were not a reason to break their monogamy agreement. Rather, if a sexual problem occurred, it was a cue to address the problem and reinforce desire/pleasure/eroticism/satisfaction. Monogamy is not a major factor in marital satisfaction and security, but conflicts over monogamy or secrecy destabilize your relationship.

## Sasha and Elliott

A secret EMA, whether by the man or woman, is a major crisis for the relationship. Sasha had fallen in love with a work colleague. After five months, this turned into a secret EMA. Friends at work saw this coming, but Sasha hadn't. She thought it would remain a "special friendship" since Sasha was committed to Elliott and her family (children 11, 9, and 6). The transition to a sexual EMA was not intentional, but a series of seductive touching which broke boundaries. Sasha found this very powerful, and her attempts to set new boundaries could not match the emotional and sexual pull of the lover relationship. Surprisingly, when they began having intercourse the dramatic emotional pull was lessened, but at that point the EMA was fully in control. In retrospect, Sasha felt the sexual pull was most powerful before the EMA was consummated.

For the next nine weeks Sasha felt torn and distressed by a roller coaster of emotions. On one hand, she was a caring wife with family responsibilities. On the other hand, she was in the whirlpool of a dramatic comparison EMA and felt swept away by these feelings. She tried to avoid Elliott, but felt guilty, which drove an increase in marital sex

(Elliott was pleased by Sasha's sexual intensity). Sasha had not imagined she could be sexually responsive with her lover and her husband. The sexual experiences were a mix of powerful emotions, erotic intensity, and guilt. Sasha felt badly for Elliott, especially his reactions to her sexual responsivity.

Work EMAs are particularly vulnerable to gossip and exposure. Although there was not a supervisory dimension to Sasha's EMA relationship, they did have overlapping duties. A female co-worker suspected something romantic/sexual was occurring. This began a quickly increasing cycle of gossip. Elliot told Sasha he'd received an anonymous e-mail about her work relationship, which panicked Sasha.

EMAs are easier to get into than out of. This is particularly true of female comparison EMAs in a work setting. The affair partner blamed Sasha for the situation and told the supervisor to drop Sasha from a project. Several people became involved and Sasha received unsettling phone calls at home, including one from a work colleague threatening to tell Elliott. Sasha realized the news of the EMA would be better coming from her than someone else. She asked her sister to babysit and invited Elliott for a walk in the park. Sasha didn't know what to expect when she told Elliott she'd fallen into an EMA, but certainly didn't expect him to cry. Elliott was shocked and couldn't believe that he'd met the EMA partner and that his wife had been attracted to that man.

Rather than attack Elliott or defend the affair partner, Sasha took responsibility for the EMA and told Elliott that she needed his help to end the EMA. She had done an internet search for marriage friendly therapists and asked if she scheduled a couple consultation whether Elliott would attend. Like intimacy and sexuality, an EMA is best understood and dealt with as a couple issue. Elliott valued their marriage and family. The disclosure of the EMA resulted in a post-traumatic stress disorder (PTSD) for Elliot. The couple therapist was empathic and respectful. She realized there were five clients to attend to: (1) Sasha, (2) Elliott, (3) their general relationship, (4) their sexual relationship, and (5) their couple history, especially the EMA. Rather than drama and blame—counter-blame, the therapist urged Sasha and Elliott to make genuine meaning of the EMA. You can learn from the past, but cannot change the past. Your power for change is in the present and future.

A crucial therapeutic intervention was discussing what Elliott could do to help Sasha end the EMA. This intervention was rehearsed in the therapist's office. Sasha and Elliott invited the EMA partner to their house for lunch. No drama and no alcohol, but a clear message that Sasha and Elliott were in couple therapy and committed to their marriage. To use a favorite analogy, they were "reopening emotional and sexual windows while walling off the EMA partner". They made it clear that Sasha would not accept phone calls, e-mails, or personal contact with the ex-lover. Sasha and Elliott would have a short weekly check-in to ensure there was not a regression. Sasha had considered changing jobs, but realized this would be an "emotional choice", not a wise decision. Elliott concurred that they shouldn't give the EMA more power than it deserved.

Sasha and Elliott engaged in a personal, specific dialogue in therapy and at home about whether they would commit to a new, strong trust and monogamy agreement. There were two parts to their change commitment. The first was to develop a new couple sexual style which integrated desire/pleasure/eroticism/satisfaction. The second was a relapse prevention agreement (based on the traditional monogamy exercise in the next section). More important than a genuine apology for the EMA was Sasha's commitment to building a new trust bond and couple sexual style.

## Claude and Madison

When they married 13 years ago, Claude and Madison began as a traditional monogamous couple, which they affirmed in a religious marriage ceremony. However, like most traditional couples, there was not a dialogue about what monogamy meant and how to create an EMA prevention plan.

Madison and Claude valued their marriage and family. They had a functional sexual relationship in terms of arousal and orgasm, but sex was infrequent (two to three times a month) and neither vital nor satisfying.

Claude masturbated two to three times a week and was turned-on by fantasies of young women who loved giving oral sex and receiving hard-driving intercourse. Madison fantasized about a lover who she would meet three to four times a year for a romantic, sexual weekend. Neither of their fantasy EMAs were meant to threaten the marriage.

It was Claude who encouraged Madison to actualize her fantasy. Claude's hope was that having a sexy weekend with a lover would increase her enthusiasm for sex with him. His hope was not realized. For Madison, the lover experience weakened her desire for marital sex. Her EMA did have the effect of Madison giving Elliott permission to have fun sex with younger women if he maintained red lines about using condoms and not falling in love. Madison and Elliott developed a "monogamish" marriage. They reinforced a solid commitment to their marriage. Elliott valued marital sex more than Madison. Madison loved Elliott as a spouse and the father of her children, but sexually preferred the occasional get together with her lover. Elliott valued the dramatic sex of his high opportunity EMAs as well as valuing his marriage and the stability of their family. Monogamish sexuality provided an erotic charge that did not destabilize them or their marriage.

### Exercise: Your Couple Monogamy Agreement

Most couples affirm monogamy to promote intimacy and security. This exercise asks you to take good words and intentions and translate this to a personally relevant, specific EMA prevention plan. There are three components to the monogamy plan.

First, be honest with yourself. Be aware of the type of person, situation, and mood which would make you vulnerable to an EMA. We believe all people and all relationships have vulnerabilities. Awareness of personal vulnerabilities is the first step in prevention. For example, you might be vulnerable to a needy person, a group setting where you feel marginalized, or maybe the situation is being lonely or feeling you want to help someone. Rather than feeling badly or guilty about your vulnerabilities, share these with your spouse so both of you are aware.

Second, if the situation poses an elevated risk for EMA, share this with your partner rather than acting it out or feeling bad or guilty about your vulnerability. Treat a potential EMA as you would any important life decision (buying a house, having a second child, changing jobs). Dialogue about the impact of an EMA on you, your partner, and your relationship.

Third, if there is an EMA incident (in person or on-line, intercourse or erotic touching) disclose it within 72 hours. Do not keep it secret. Covering up adds to feelings of betrayal which are more powerful than the EMA itself.

This monogamy agreement is not based on fear or being a sexual detective. The foundation is valuing the intimacy and security of your relationship, especially couple sexuality. Monogamy requires an honest dialogue about personal, situational, relational, and sexual vulnerabilities. Monogamy is a couple commitment based on a positive influence process.

### Alternative Exercise: Consensual Non-Monogamy Agreement

An agreement regarding non-traditional values is even more important than a traditional EMA agreement. You've decided on CNM. You want to be sure that sexuality has a 15–20% positive role in your life and relationship. Your CNM agreement has three components.

First, be clear what you value, both emotionally and sexually, about your marital (partnered) relationship. This can include family, social acceptance, a place in the community, financial stability, a friendship, an affectionate bond.

Second, be clear about what type of CNM is good for your sexual life and does not destabilize your primary relationship. There are major differences between an open relationship, a swinging relationship, and polyamory relationships. For example, in open relationships (the most common type of EMA) the erotic charge is generated by a new sex partner and scenario. With swinging relationships, the excitement involves creating ongoing sexual friendships and new boundaries, including whether you are present when your partner is sexual with others. Polyamory relationships allow you to form a community involving emotional and sexual connection with other individuals and couples. Choose the type of CNM which is the right fit for you and facilitates your sexual needs.

Third, the issue of boundaries. What are the red lines which would be destructive for you and CNM? Examples include getting pregnant, falling in love with the CNM partner, contracting an STI/HIV, being sexual with a brother-in-law or your spouse's best friend, or a work relationship which subverts your career.

If you decide on a CNM agreement, you owe it to yourself to play this out in a way which promotes your authentic sexual self so that sexuality has a positive role in your life and relationship(s).

## Summary

Sexuality is not the most important aspect of a marriage (relationship), but sexual conflicts can have an inordinately powerful destabilizing effect. This is particularly true of secret EMAs. Traditionally, couples assumed monogamy. When the EMA was discovered, it powerfully affected the injured partner (PTSD response) and threatened the relationship. In the culture, EMAs were almost universally judged as wrong. The rules were clear, although often broken.

Some believe we should go back to the old days of assuming monogamy and not discussing it. We totally disagree. Monogamy needs to be carefully considered. If you and your spouse decide on monogamy (which is the most common decision for married, partnered, cohabitating, and lesbian couples), you need a specific agreement to promote monogamy and prevent EMAs.

Couples with non-traditional values decide to utilize CNM. Ideally, this is a careful decision which promotes sexual vitality without destabilizing the person or your primary relationship. Being opposed to traditional monogamy is not enough. You need a clear strategy which enhances sexuality and is not destructive for you or your primary relationship.

Do not fall into a "right—wrong" power struggle where you demonize other people and their values. Decide what is right for you and your relationship so that your agreement promotes desire/pleasure/eroticism/satisfaction.

# Appendix A

# CHOOSING A SEX, COUPLE, OR INDIVIDUAL THERAPIST

This is a self-help book, not a do-it-yourself therapy book. Many individuals and couples are reluctant to consult a therapist, feeling that to do so is a sign of weakness, a confession of inadequacy, or an admission that their life and relationship are in dire straits. In reality, seeking professional help means that you realize there is a problem. You have made a commitment to address the issues and promote individual, couple, and sexual growth.

The mental health field can be confusing. Couple therapy and sex therapy are clinical subspecialties. They are offered by several professionals—psychologists, marital therapists, pastoral counselors, psychiatrists, social workers, and licensed professional counselors. The professional background of the clinician is less important than her competence in dealing with sexual, couple, and individual problems.

Many people have health insurance that provides coverage for mental health; thus, they can afford the services of a private practice therapist. Those who have neither the financial resources nor insurance could consider a university or medical school outpatient mental health clinic, a family services center, or a public mental health clinic. Most clinics have a sliding fee scale program.

When choosing a therapist, be direct in asking about credentials and areas of expertise. Ask the clinician what the focus of therapy will be, how long therapy is expected to last, and whether the emphasis is specifically on sexual problems or on individual, communication, or relationship issues. Be especially diligent in asking about university degrees and licensing. There are poorly qualified persons—and some outright quacks—in any field.

One of the best ways to obtain a referral is to call or look on-line for a professional organization such as a state psychological association, marriage and family therapy association, or mental health association. You can ask for a referral from a family physician, minister, imam, rabbi, or a trusted friend. If you live near a university or medical school, call to find what specialized psychological or sexual health services may be available.

For a sex therapy referral, contact the American Association of Sex Educators, Counselors, and Therapists (AASECT) at www.aasect.org. Another resource is the Society for Sex Therapy and Research (SSTAR) at https://sstarnet.org.

For a marital therapist, check the on-line site for the American Association for Marriage and Family Therapy (AAMFT) at https://therapist-locator.net.

If you are looking for a psychologist who can provide individual or couple therapy for anxiety, depression, behavioral health, and other issues, we suggest the National Registry of Health Service Providers in Psychology at www.findapsychologist.org.

Feel free to speak with two or three therapists before deciding with whom to work. Be aware of your level of comfort and degree of rapport with the therapist as well as whether the therapist's assessment of the problem and approach to treatment make sense to you. Once you begin, give therapy a chance to be helpful. There are few miracle cures. Change requires commitment; it is a gradual and often difficult process. Although many people benefit from short-term therapy (less than ten sessions), most find the therapeutic process will require four months or longer. The role of the therapist is that of consultant rather than the decision-maker. Therapy requires effort on your part, both during the sessions and between sessions. Therapy helps you change attitudes, behaviors, and feelings. It takes courage to seek professional assistance. Therapy can be a tremendous help in assessing and ameliorating sexual, couple, and individual problems.

# Appendix B

# SUGGESTED READINGS

## Suggested Readings on Couple Sexuality

McCarthy, B. & McCarthy, E. (2009). Discovering your couple sexual style. New York: Routledge.
McCarthy, B. & McCarthy, E. (2012). Sexual awareness (5th ed.). New York: Routledge.
McCarthy, B. & McCarthy, E. (2014). Rekindling desire (2nd ed.). New York: Routledge.
Metz, M. & McCarthy, B. (2010). Enduring desire. New York: Routledge.
Perel, E. (2006). Mating in captivity. New York: Harper Collins.
Snyder, S. (2018). Love worth making. New York: St. Martin's.

## Suggested Readings on Relationship Satisfaction

de Marneffee, D. (2018). The rough patch. New York: Scribner.
Doherty, W. (2013). Take back your marriage (2nd ed.). New York: Guilford.
Finkel, E. (2017). The all-or-nothing marriage. New York: Dutton.
Gottman, J. & Silver, N. (2015). The seven principles for making marriage work (2nd ed.). New York: Harmony.
Johnson, S. (2008). Hold me tight. Boston: Little, Brown.
Love, P. & Stosny, S. (2008). How to improve your marriage without talking about it. New York: Three Rivers.
Markman, H., Stanley, S., & Blumberg, S. (2010). Fighting for your marriage (3rd ed.) San Francisco: Jossey-Bass.
McCarthy, B. & McCarthy, E. (2004). Getting it right the first time. New York: Routledge.
McCarthy, B. & McCarthy, E. (2006). Getting it right this time. New York: Routledge.

## Suggested Readings on Female Sexuality

Brotto, L. (2018). Better sex through mindfulness. New York: Greystone.
Foley, S., Kope, S., & Sugrue, D. (2012). Sex matters for women (2nd ed.). New York: Guilford.

Heiman, J. & LoPiccolo, J. (1998). Becoming orgasmic. New York: Prentice-Hall.
McCarthy, B. & McCarthy, E. (2019). Finding your sexual voice. New York: Routledge.
Nagoski, E. (2015). Come as you are. New York: Simon and Schuster.

## Suggested Readings on Male Sexuality

McCarthy, B. & Metz, M. (2008). Men's sexual health. New York: Routledge.
Metz, M. & McCarthy, B. (2003). Coping with premature ejaculation. Oakland, CA.: New Harbinger.
Metz, M. & McCarthy, B. (2004). Coping with erectile dysfunction. Oakland, CA.: New Harbinger.
Zilbergeld, B. (1999). The new male sexuality. New York: Bantam.

## Other Significant Sexuality Readings

Maltz, W. (2012). The sexual healing journey (3rd ed.). New York: William Morrow.
Michael, R., Gagnon, J., Laumann, E., & Kolata, G. (1994). Sex in America. Boston: Little, Brown.
Snyder, D., Baucom, D., & Gordon, K. (2007). Getting past the affair. New York: Guilford.

# REFERENCES

Ahlborg, T. (2008). Sensual and sexual marital contentment in parents of small children. Journal of Sex Research, 45, 295–304.
Allen, E., Adkins, D., Baucom, D., Snyder, D., & Glass, S. (2005). Intrapersonal, interpersonal, and contextual factors in engaging in and response to extramarital involvement. Clinical Psychology: Science and Practice, 12, 101–130.
Althof, S. (2014). Treatment of premature ejaculation. In Y. Binik & K. Hall (Eds.) Principles and practice of sex therapy (5th ed., pp. 42–60). New York: Guilford.
Barbach, L. (1975). For yourself. New York: Doubleday.
Baucom, D., Pentel, K., Gordon, K. & Snyder, D. (2017). An integrative approach to treating infidelity in couples. In J. Fitzgerald (Ed.) Foundations for couples' therapy (pp. 206–215). New York: Routledge.
Binik, Y. & Hall, K. (2014). Principles and practice of sex therapy (5th ed.). New York: Routledge.
Boney-McCoy, S. & Finkelhor, D. (1995). Psychosocial sequelae of violent victimization in a national youth sample. Journal of Consulting and Clinical Psychology, 63, 725–736.
Brotto, L. (2018). Better sex through mindfulness. New York: Greystone.
Byers, L. & Rehman, V. (2014). Sexual well-being. In D. Tolman & L. Diamond (Eds.) APA handbook of sexuality and psychology. Vol. 1 (pp. 317–337). Washington, DC: American Psychological Association.
Epstein, N. & Falconier, M. (2017). Shame in couple relationships. In J. Fitzgerald (Ed.) Foundations for couples' therapy. (pp. 374–383). New York: Routledge.
Fine, M. & Harvey, M. (2006). Handbook of divorce and relationship dissolution. Hillsdale, NJ: Erlbaum.
Finkel, E. (2017). The all-or-none marriage. New York: Dutton.
Foley, S., Kope, S., & Sugrue, D. (2012). Sex matters for women (2nd ed.). New York: Guilford.
Frank, E., Anderson, A., & Rubinstein, D. (1978). Frequency of sexual dysfunction in "normal" couples. New England Journal of Medicine, 299, 111–115.
Gillespie, B. (2017). Correlates of sexual frequency and satisfaction among partnered older adults. Journal of Sex and Marital Therapy, 43, 403–421.

# REFERENCES

Girard, A. & Woolley, S. (2017). Using emotionally focused therapy to treat sexual desire discrepancy in couples. Journal of Sex and Marital Therapy, 43, 720–735.
Glass, S. (2003). Not "Just Friends". New York: Free Press.
Gordon, K., Baucom, D., & Snyder, D. (2004). An integrative intervention promoting recovery from extramarital affairs. Journal of Marriage and Family Therapy, 36, 213–231.
Gottman, J. & Silver, N. (2015). The seven principles for making marriage work (2nd ed.). New York: Harmony.
Graham, C. (2014). Orgasm disorders in women. In Y. Binik & K. Hall (Eds.). Principles and practice of sex therapy (5th ed., pp. 89–111). New York: Guilford.
Hyde, J. (2005). The gender similarities hypothesis. American Psychologist, 60, 581–592.
Impett, E., Peplau, L., & Gable, S. (2005). Approach and avoidance sexual motives. Personal Relationships, 12, 465–482.
Johnson, S. (2008). Hold me tight. Boston: Little, Brown.
Kleinplatz, P. (2010). Desire disorders or opportunities for optimal erotic intimacy. In S. Leiblum (Ed.). Treating sexual desire disorders (pp. 93–113). New York: Guilford.
Laumann, E., Gagnon, J., Michael, R., & Michaels, S. (1994). The social organization of sexuality. Chicago: University of Chicago Press.
Leiblum, S. (2002). After sildenafil: Bridging the gap between pharmacological treatment and satisfying sexual relationships. Journal of Clinical Psychiatry, 63, 17–22.
Leitenberg, H. & Henning, K. (1995). Sexual fantasy. Psychological Bulletin, 117, 469–496.
Lindau, S., Schuman, L., Laumann, E., Levenson, W., O'Muircheartaigh, C., & Waite, L. (2007). A study of sexuality and health among older adults in the United States, New England Journal of Medicine, 357, 762–764.
Maltz, W. (2012). The sexual healing journey (3rd ed.). New York: William Morrow.
Mark, K., Hebernick, D., Fortenberry, D., Sanders, S., & Reece, M. (2014). The object of sexual desire. Journal of Sexual Medicine, 11, 2709–2719.
McCarthy, B. (2002). Sexual secrets, trauma, and dysfunction. Journal of Sex and Marital Therapy, 28, 353–359.
McCarthy, B. (2015). Sex made simple. Eau Claire, WI.: PESI publications.
McCarthy, B., Koman, C., & Cohn, D. (2018). A psychosocial model for assessment, treatment, and relapse prevention for female sexual interest/arousal disorder. Sexual and Relationship Therapy, 33, 353–363.
McCarthy, B. & McCarthy, E. (2004). Getting it right the first time. New York: Routledge.
McCarthy, B. & McCarthy, E. (2009). Discovering your couple sexual style. New York: Routledge.
McCarthy, B. & McCarthy, E. (2012). Sexual awareness (5th ed.). New York: Routledge.
McCarthy, B. & McCarthy, E. (2014). Rekindling desire (2nd ed.). New York: Routledge.
McCarthy, B. & Metz, M. (2008). The "Good Enough Sex" model: A case study. Sexual and Relationship Therapy, 23, 227–234.
McCarthy, B. & Pierpaoli, C. (2015). Sexual challenges with aging. Journal of Sex and Marital Therapy, 41, 72–78.
McCarthy, B. & Ross, L. (2017). Integrating sexual concepts and interventions into couple therapy. In J. Fitzgerald (Ed.). Foundations for couples' therapy (pp. 355–364). New York: Routledge.

# REFERENCES

McCarthy, B. & Wald, L. (2017). Psychobiosocial approach to sex therapy. In Z. Peterson (Ed.) The Wiley handbook of sex therapy (pp. 190–201). Hoboken, NJ: Wiley-Blackwell.

Meana, M. (2010). When love and sex go wrong. In Levine, C. Risen, & S. Althof (Eds.) Handbook of clinical sexuality for mental health professionals (2nd ed., pp. 103–120). New York: Routledge.

Meston, C., Rellini, A., & Heiman, J. (2006). Women's history of sexual abuse, their sexuality, and sexual self-schemas. Journal of Consulting and Clinical Psychology, 74, 229–236.

Metz, M., Epstein, N., & McCarthy, B. (2017). Cognitive-behavioral therapy for sexual dysfunction. New York: Routledge.

Metz, M. & McCarthy, B. (2003). Coping with premature ejaculation. Oakland, CA.: New Harbinger.

Metz, M. & McCarthy, B. (2004). Coping with erectile dysfunction. Oakland, CA.: New Harbinger.

Metz, M. & McCarthy, B. (2010). Enduring desire. New York: Routledge.

Metz, M. & McCarthy, B. (2012). The Good Enough Sex (GES) model. In P. Kleinplatz (Ed.). New directions in sex therapy (2nd ed., pp. 212–230). New York: Routledge.

Mosher, D. (1980). Three psychological dimensions of depth of involvement in human sexual response. Journal of Sex Research, 16, 1–40.

Nagoski, E. (2015). Come as you are. New York: Simon and Schuster.

Pascoal, P., Byers, E., Alvarez, M., Santos-Iglesias, P., Nobre, P., Pereira, C., & Laan, E. (2017). A dyadic approach to understanding the link between sexual function and sexual satisfaction in heterosexual couples. Journal of Sex Research, 55, 1155–1166.

Perel, E. (2006). Mating in captivity. New York: HarperCollins.

Perel, E. (2017). The state of affairs. New York: HarperCollins.

Rellini, A. (2014). The treatment of sexual dysfunction in survivors of sexual abuse. In Y. Binik & K. Hall (Eds.) Principles and practice of sex therapy (5th ed., pp. 375–398). New York: Guilford.

Renaud, C. & Byers, E. (2001). Positive and negative sexual cognitions. Journal of Sex Research, 38, 252–262.

Tennov, D. (1998). Love and limerance. New York: Scarborough.

Weiner, L. & Avery-Clark, C. (2017). Sensate focus in sex therapy. New York: Routledge.

Zilbergeld, B. (1999). The new male sexuality. New York: Bantam.

For Product Safety Concerns and Information please contact our EU representative GPSR@taylorandfrancis.com
Taylor & Francis Verlag GmbH, Kaufingerstraße 24, 80331 München, Germany

www.ingramcontent.com/pod-product-compliance
Lightning Source LLC
Chambersburg PA
CBHW051541230426

43669CB00015B/2678